ACTIVITIES FOR LITTLE LEARNERS

PRESCHOOL & KINDERGARTEN

CREATIVE GAMES, CRAFTS, PUPPETS, PUZZLES, LEARNING WHEELS AND MUCH MORE!

CREATED AND ILLUSTRATED BY KAREN FINCH
FINCH FAMILY GAMES

FINCH FAMILY GAMES PUBLICATIONS

CREATED AND ILLUSTRATED
BY
KAREN FINCH

Copyright ©1994 by Finch Family Games
All rights reserved.
Printed in the United States of America
Published by Finch Family Games Publications
10821 North 5750 West
Highland, Utah 84003

ISBN 1-885476-00-0

HOW TO USE THIS BOOK:

THIS BOOK HAS BEEN DESIGNED FOR TEACHERS, HOME SCHOOLS AND FAMILIES IN TEACHING AND ENHANCING THE LEARNING ATMOSPHERE YEAR ROUND. THIS BOOK WAS CREATED ESPECIALLY FOR THE PRESCHOOL AND KINDERGARTEN AGE CHILDREN, BUT CAN EASILY BE USED FOR YOUNGER OR SLIGHTLY OLDER CHILDREN AS WELL. INCLUDED ARE FUN GAMES, ACTIVITIES, PUZZLES, PUPPETS, CRAFTS, AND MUCH MORE! EACH PROJECT HAS BEEN DESIGNED FOR FUN AND ENJOYMENT AS WELL AS SKILL DEVELOPMENT. KEEP THIS BOOK AS YOUR MASTER BY MAKING COPIES FROM THE PAGES. IF PIECES FROM A GAME ARE LOST, YOU WILL HAVE A COPY FROM WHICH TO REPRODUCE THE LOST ITEM. PLEASE DO NOT MAKE COPIES OF THIS BOOK TO GIVE TO OTHER TEACHERS, FAMILIES, OR FRIENDS. ENCOURAGE THESE INDIVIDUALS TO PURCHASE THEIR OWN BOOKS.

THE FOLLOWING BASIC MATERIALS AND CONSTRUCTION INFORMATION WILL BE USEFUL IN COMPLETING THE GAMES AND LEARNING WHEELS IN THIS BOOK.

1. COPY AND MOUNT EACH PAGE ON A HEAVIER CARDSTOCK OR POSTER-TYPE MATERIAL. THIS WILL INCREASE THE LIFE OF YOUR VISUALS.

2. COLOR USING WATERCOLOR MARKERS AND PASTEL CHALKS. THE MARKERS GIVE BRIGHT, VIVID COLOR AND THE PASTELS GIVE THE SOFTER VALUES YOU MAY NEED WITH SOME PICTURES. DO NOT USE CRAYONS. THEY WILL MELT WHEN LAMINATED AND WILL SPREAD BEYOND THE COLORING LINES.

3. LAMINATE ALL CARDS, GAMES, FOLDERS, LEARNING WHEELS, ETC. THIS WILL PREVENT ANYTHING FROM SMEARING OR RUINING YOUR VISUAL AND WILL MAKE YOUR PROJECT MORE DURABLE.

4. A FUN PRODUCT CALLED "STICKY-BACK" VELCRO CAN BE USED ON ANY LAMINATED SURFACE TO HOLD PIECES ON. THIS ELIMINATES THE NEED FOR USING TAPE OVER AND OVER AGAIN. "STICKY-BACK" VELCRO CAN BE PURCHASED AT ANY FABRIC OR CRAFT STORE.

**This book is dedicated to the
memory of a loving father**

TABLE OF CONTENTS

"RE-USEABLE ACTIVITY BOOK"

RE-USEABLE ACTIVITY BOOKS ARE A MUST FOR ANY CLASSROOM LEARNING CENTER, INDIVIDUAL CHILD'S ACTIVITY BOX, OR FOR HOME REENFORCEMENT AND LEARNING. SINCE THESE BOOKS ARE FULLY LAMINATED, CHILDREN CAN DO THE ACTIVITIES ON EACH PAGE OVER AND OVER AGAIN BY USING CRAYONS. THE CRAYONS CAN BE EASILY WIPED OFF WITH TISSUE PAPER OR A SMALL CLOTH.

<u>HOW TO MAKE:</u> REPRODUCE EACH PAGE OF THE ACTIVITY BOOK ONTO A WHITE CARDSTOCK. CUT OUT EACH PAGE ALONG THE DARK OUTSIDE LINES. LAMINATE EACH PAGE. PUNCH TWO HOLES ON THE TOP OF EACH PAGE AND HOLD BOOK TOGETHER WITH RINGS AS SHOWN. REPRODUCE THE COVER PAGE ONTO A HEAVIER CARDSTOCK. COLOR, CUT AND LAMINATE COVER. THE INSIDE PAGES WILL NOT BE COLORED. USE REGULAR CRAYONS OR SPECIALLY MADE "WIPE CRAYONS" WHICH CAN BE PURCHASED AT ANY SCHOOL SUPPLY STORE.

FOLLOW THE DOTS
ONE BY ONE...
YOU'LL DRAW SOMETHING
THAT'S LOTS OF FUN!!

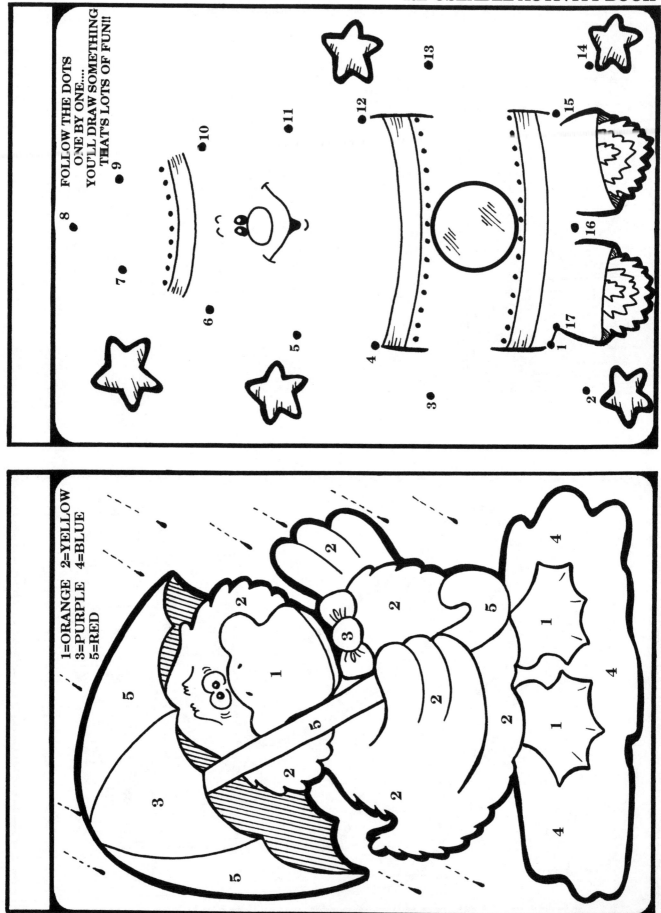

1=ORANGE   2=YELLOW
3=PURPLE   4=BLUE
5=RED

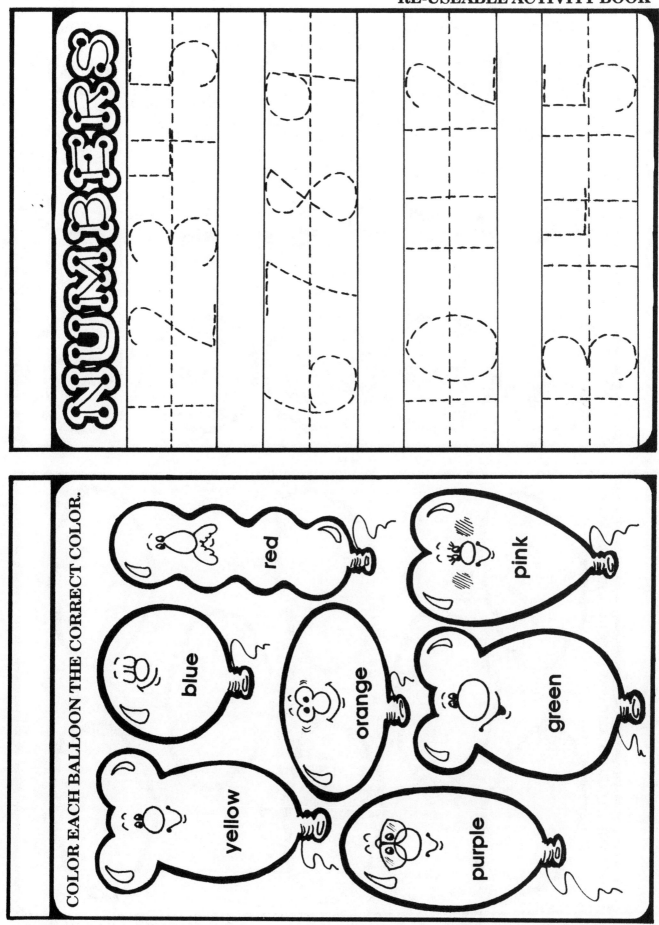

NUMBERS

COLOR EACH BALLOON THE CORRECT COLOR.

red

pink

blue

orange

green

yellow

purple

FINCH FAMILY GAMES ©1994

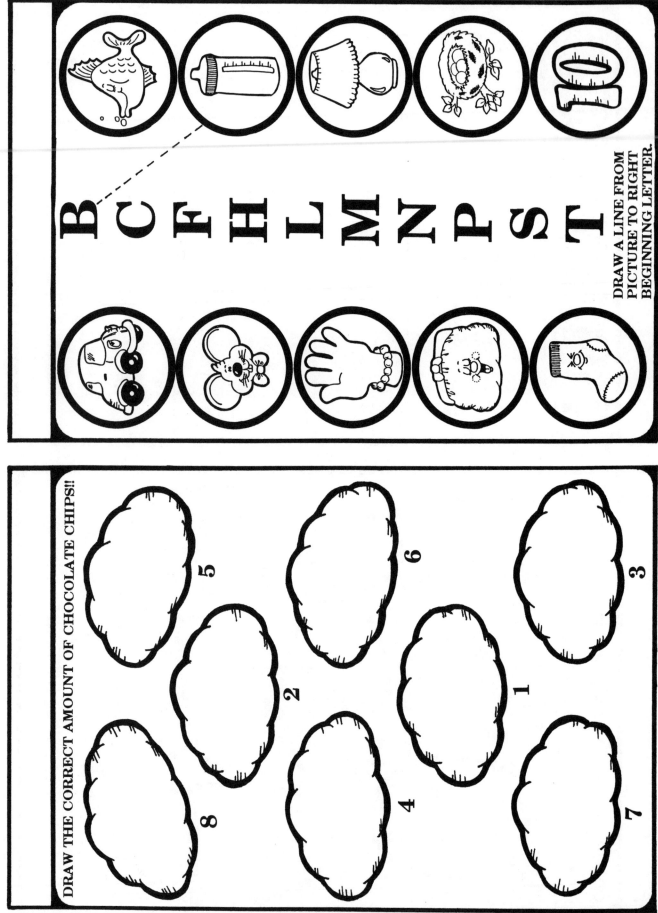

DRAW A LINE FROM PICTURE TO RIGHT BEGINNING LETTER.

B
C
F
H
L
M
N
P
S
T

DRAW THE CORRECT AMOUNT OF CHOCOLATE CHIPS!!

TRACE AND MATCH THE SHAPES TO THE PICTURES.

FINISH THE PICTURE!

LETTERS

abcde
fghij
klmn
opqrst
uvwxyz

BUZZZZZZZZZ

TRACE AND COLOR

"EVERYONE 'CHIP' IN ACTIVITY"

HOW TO USE: REPRODUCE AS MANY OF THESE COOKIES AS YOU NEED. ON THE CENTER OF EACH COOKIE WRITE A JOB OR TASK. WHEN IT IS TIME TO CLEAN UP, EACH CHILD WILL PICK A COOKIE AND DO THE JOB INDICATED ON IT. WHEN THE JOB IS COMPLETED, PUT THE COOKIE IN THE MOUTH OF EITHER THE BOY OR GIRL VISUAL. THE CHILD WHO "CHIPS" IN THE MOST WILL RECEIVE THE "I 'CHIPPED' IN TODAY!" NECKLACE. IT MIGHT BE FUN TO HAVE A CHOCOLATE CHIP COOKIE PARTY AT THE END OF THE WEEK OR MONTH TO GO ALONG WITH THIS ACTIVITY.

*WHEN WORKING WITH YOUNG CHILDREN, SIMPLY WRITE THEIR NAMES ON EACH COOKIE INSTEAD OF A JOB. WHEN THEY HAVE DONE THE JOB YOU HAVE TOLD THEM TO DO, THEN THEY CAN FIND THEIR OWN COOKIE AND PLACE IT IN THE BOY OR GIRL BOX.

FINCH FAMILY GAMES © 1994

*REPRODUCE THIS PAGE AND THEN COLOR AND CUT IT OUT. CUT OUT AREA INSIDE MOUTH. LAMINATE FOR DURABILITY. PREPARE A CEREAL BOX BY COVERING WITH BUTCHER PAPER. PLACE FACE ON BOX AND PENCIL IN WHERE HOLE IN MOUTH WILL BE. REMOVE FACE AND CUT OUT PENCILED HOLE. ATTACH FACE TO FRONT OF BOX SO THAT HOLE IN BOX AND HOLE IN MOUTH MATCH UP.

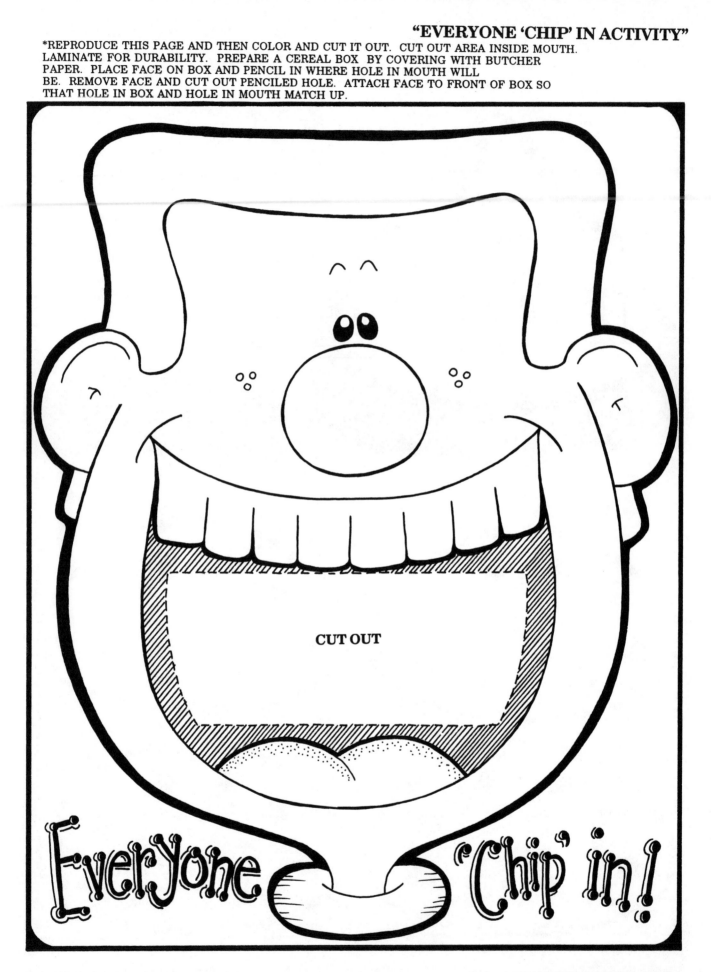

CUT OUT

FINCH FAMILY GAMES ©1994

*REPRODUCE THIS PAGE AND THEN COLOR AND CUT IT OUT. CUT OUT AREA INSIDE MOUTH. LAMINATE FOR DURABILITY. PREPARE A CEREAL BOX BY COVERING WITH BUTCHER PAPER. PLACE FACE ON BOX AND PENCIL IN WHERE HOLE IN MOUTH WILL BE. REMOVE FACE AND CUT OUT PENCILED HOLE. ATTACH FACE TO FRONT OF BOX SO THAT HOLE IN BOX AND HOLE IN MOUTH MATCH UP.

CUT OUT

Everyone 'Chip' in!

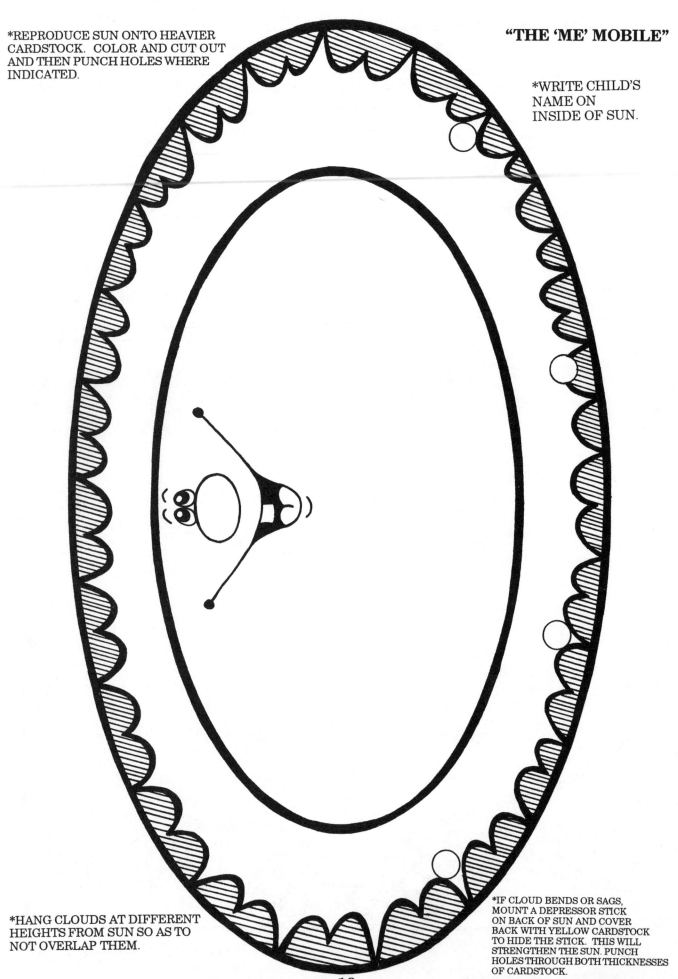

*REPRODUCE SUN ONTO HEAVIER CARDSTOCK. COLOR AND CUT OUT AND THEN PUNCH HOLES WHERE INDICATED.

*WRITE CHILD'S NAME ON INSIDE OF SUN.

*HANG CLOUDS AT DIFFERENT HEIGHTS FROM SUN SO AS TO NOT OVERLAP THEM.

*IF CLOUD BENDS OR SAGS, MOUNT A DEPRESSOR STICK ON BACK OF SUN AND COVER BACK WITH YELLOW CARDSTOCK TO HIDE THE STICK. THIS WILL STRENGTHEN THE SUN. PUNCH HOLES THROUGH BOTH THICKNESSES OF CARDSTOCK.

*REPRODUCE THESE CLOUDS ONTO A WHITE CARDSTOCK. COLOR AND CUT OUT EACH CLOUD. PUNCH HOLES IN THE TOP OF EACH CLOUD.

*COLOR EACH CRAYON A FAVORITE COLOR.

MY FAVORITE COLORS

*DRAW THE CORRECT AMOUNT OF CANDLES ON THE CAKE FOR YOUR AGE. WRITE IN THE CORRECT NUMBER ON THE BLANK.

I AM

_____

YEARS OLD

FINCH FAMILY GAMES © 1994

*REPRODUCE THESE CLOUDS ONTO A
WHITE CARDSTOCK. COLOR AND CUT
OUT EACH CLOUD. PUNCH HOLES IN
THE TOP OF EACH CLOUD.

*CUT OUT FAVORITE FOODS FROM
A MAGAZINE OR OLD WORKBOOK
OR HAVE CHILD DRAW FAVORITE
FOODS.

MY FAVORITE FOODS

*MOUNT THREE PHOTOS OF SPECIAL
PEOPLE OR HAVE CHILD DRAW A
FACE IN EACH PICTURE FRAME.

PEOPLE THAT ARE SPECIAL TO ME!

FINCH FAMILY GAMES ©1994

18

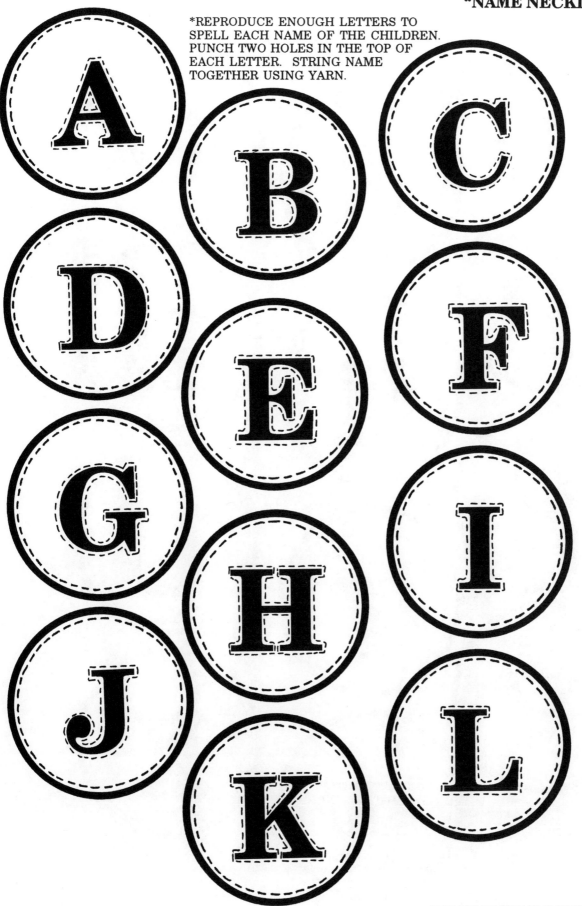

*REPRODUCE ENOUGH LETTERS TO
SPELL EACH NAME OF THE CHILDREN.
PUNCH TWO HOLES IN THE TOP OF
EACH LETTER. STRING NAME
TOGETHER USING YARN.

*REPRODUCE ENOUGH LETTERS TO
SPELL EACH NAME OF THE CHILDREN.
PUNCH TWO HOLES IN THE TOP OF
EACH LETTER. STRING NAME
TOGETHER USING YARN.

"NAME NECKLACES"

FINCH FAMILY GAMES ©1994

*REPRODUCE ENOUGH LETTERS TO
SPELL EACH NAME OF THE CHILDREN.
PUNCH TWO HOLES IN THE TOP OF
EACH LETTER. STRING NAME
TOGETHER USING YARN.

"APPLE HAT"

*REPRODUCE THE APPLES ON CONSTRUCTION PAPER. HAVE CHILDREN COLOR, CUT
OUT, AND WRITE NAME ON CENTER APPLE. STAPLE OR GLUE TO STRIP OF
CONSTRUCTION PAPER LONG ENOUGH TO GO AROUND HEAD OF CHILD.

MY NAME
IS

_____

FINCH FAMILY GAMES © 1994

IT'S TIME TO SHOUT A **BIG** HOORAY!
BECAUSE IT IS YOUR SPECIAL DAY!
I'LL DRAW A BIRTHDAY WISH FOR YOU,
AND HOPE YOUR WISHES ALL COME TRUE!

HAPPY BIRTHDAY TO YOU!
LOVE,

*REPRODUCE CARD ON HEAVIER CARDSTOCK. COLOR AND CUT OUT. FOLD EACH SIDE ON DOTTED LINE SO THAT BALLOONS ARE ON THE FRONT OF THE CARD AS SHOWN BELOW. COLOR AND CUT OUT INSIDE OF CARD. MOUNT TO INSIDE OF FOLDED CARD. DRAW A BIRTHDAY WISH IN OUTLINED BOX INSIDE CARD.

"HAPPY BIRTHDAY WRISTBAND"

*REPRODUCE ONTO HEAVIER CARDSTOCK. COLOR AND CUT OUT. PLACE AROUND CHILD'S WRIST AND TAPE TO CORRECT SIZE. GIVE THIS AS PART OF THE BIRTHDAY CELEBRATION GIFTS.

*REPRODUCE PUPPETS ONTO HEAVIER
CARDSTOCK. COLOR, CUT OUT AND
LAMINATE FOR DURABILITY. TAPE
LARGE DEPRESSOR STICK ON BACK.

FINCH FAMILY GAMES © 1994

*REPRODUCE PUPPETS ONTO HEAVIER
CARDSTOCK. COLOR, CUT OUT AND
LAMINATE FOR DURABILITY. TAPE
LARGE DEPRESSOR STICK ON BACK.

FINCH FAMILY GAMES © 1994

*REPRODUCE "LOONEY LOUIE" ONTO HEAVIER CARDSTOCK. COLOR, CUT OUT AND LAMINATE FOR DURABILITY. TAPE LARGE DEPRESSOR STICK ON BACK.

"Looney Louie" ↘

*KIDS LOVE TO LEARN WITH PUPPETS. "LOONEY LOUIE" IS A CHARACTER THAT CAN TEACH THEM THE RIGHT AND WRONG WAY OF ANY SUBJECT. CHILDREN LOVE TO HAVE SOMEONE TO CORRECT AND TEACH THE CORRECT WAY IT SHOULD BE DONE.

*PUPPET STAGES CAN BE MADE FROM A VARIETY OF THINGS. DRAPE A SHEET OVER CHAIRS AND WORK FROM BEHIND THE SHEET. BUILD A STAGE FROM A LARGE PIECE OF CARDBOARD AND FOLD IN ON THE TWO SIDES SO THAT IT WILL STAND AS SHOWN BELOW. CUT AN OPENING IN AN OLD REFRIGERATOR BOX AS SHOWN BELOW. EVERY LEARNING FILE SHOULD HAVE PUPPETS TO HELP TEACH AND BUILD BASIC SKILLS.

FINCH FAMILY GAMES ©1994

*REPRODUCE APPLE ONTO HEAVIER
CARDSTOCK. COLOR AND CUT OUT.

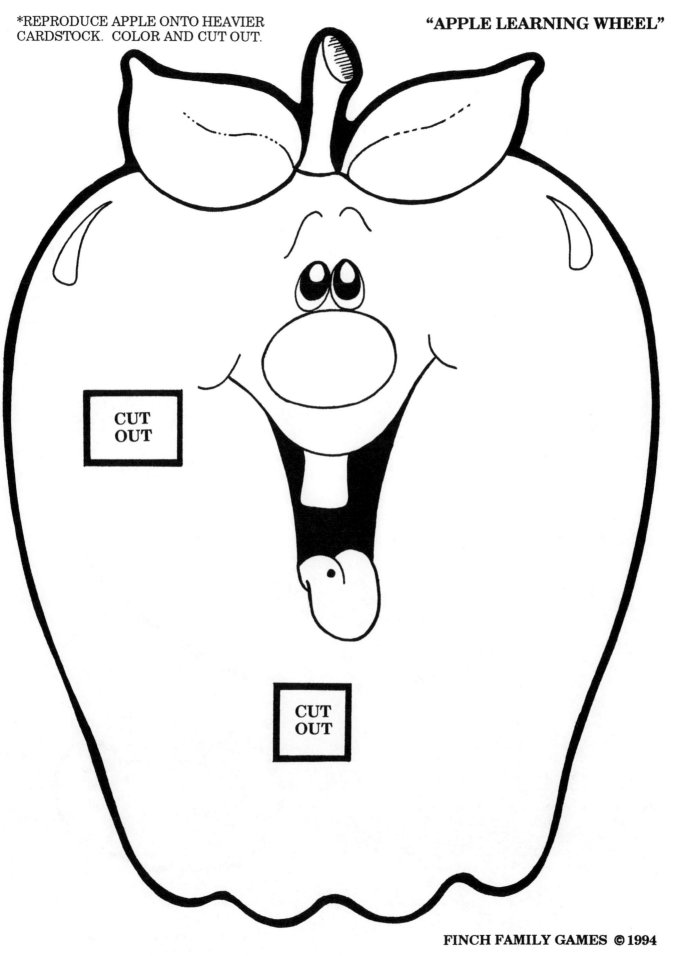

CUT
OUT

CUT
OUT

FINCH FAMILY GAMES © 1994

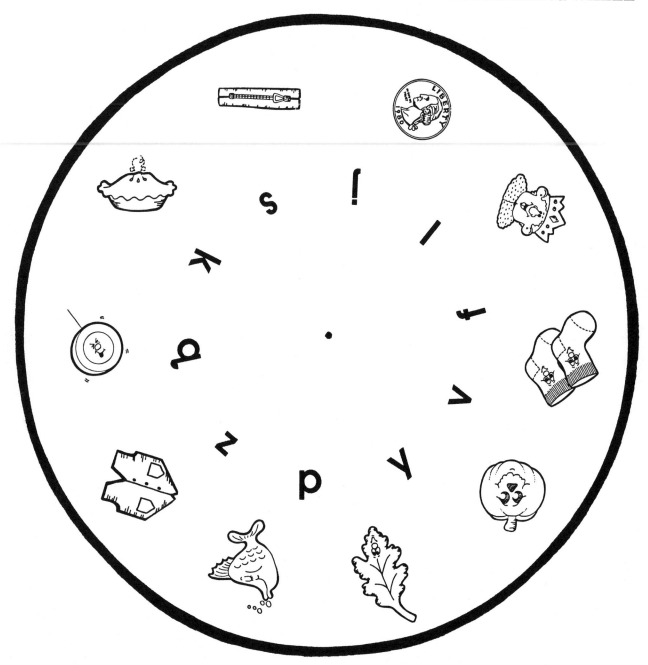

*REPRODUCE CIRCLE AND WORM ONTO HEAVIER CARDSTOCK. COLOR AND CUT OUT. POKE BRAD FASTENERS THROUGH BLACK DOTS ON APPLE, CIRCLE AND WORM. MAKE SURE PICTURES AND LETTERS ARE SHOWING THROUGH SMALL CUT OUT BOX AREAS ON APPLE. CHILD WILL MOVE WORM TO SEE IF ANSWER IS CORRECT.

FINCH FAMILY GAMES ©1994

CUT OUT

CUT OUT

*REPRODUCE CHEESE WITH MICE ONTO HEAVIER
CARDSTOCK. COLOR AND CUT OUT. CUT OUT
SMALL BOX AREAS.

FINCH FAMILY GAMES © 1994

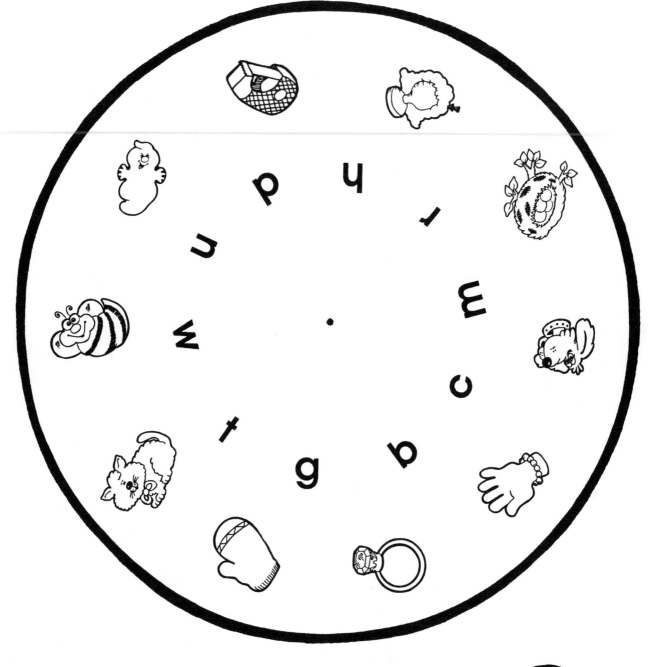

*REPRODUCE CIRCLE AND MOUSE ONTO HEAVIER CARDSTOCK. COLOR AND CUT OUT. POKE BRAD FASTENERS THROUGH BLACK DOTS ON CHEESE, MOUSE AND CIRCLE. MAKE SURE PICTURES AND LETTERS ARE SHOWING THROUGH SMALL CUT OUT BOX AREAS ON CHEESE. CHILD WILL MOVE SMALL MOUSE TO SEE IF ANSWER IS CORRECT.

FINCH FAMILY GAMES © **1994**

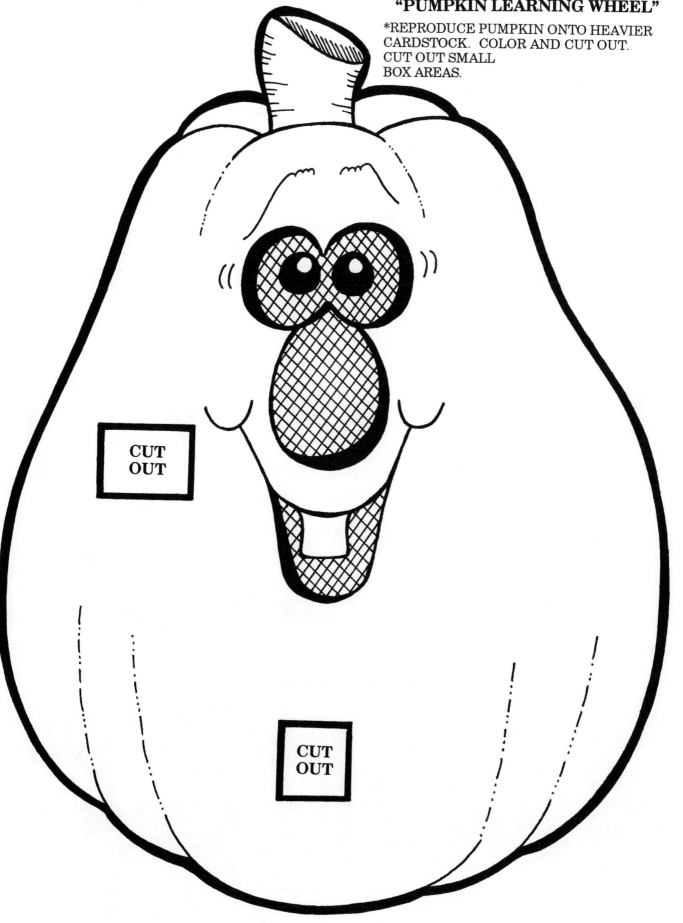

"PUMPKIN LEARNING WHEEL"

*REPRODUCE PUMPKIN ONTO HEAVIER
CARDSTOCK. COLOR AND CUT OUT.
CUT OUT SMALL
BOX AREAS.

CUT
OUT

CUT
OUT

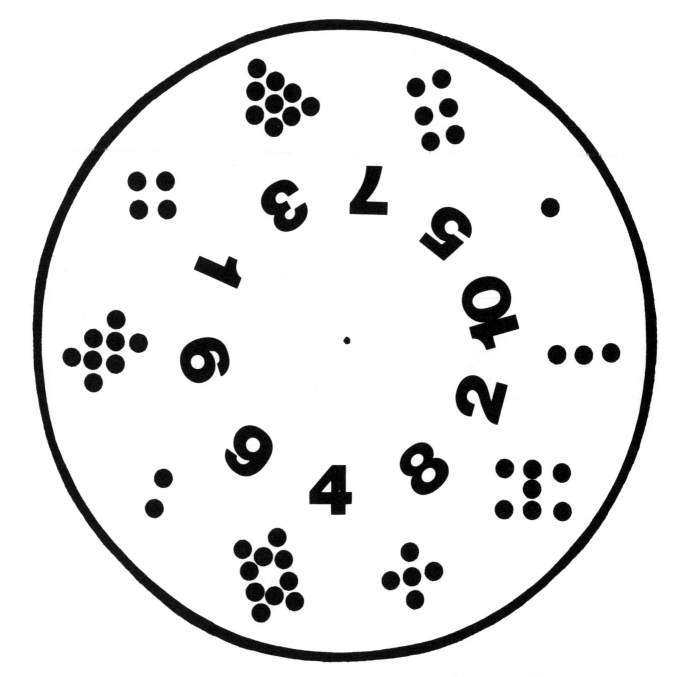

*REPRODUCE CIRCLE AND MOUSE ONTO HEAVIER CARDSTOCK. COLOR AND CUT OUT. POKE BRAD FASTENERS THROUGH BLACK DOTS ON PUMPKIN, CIRCLE AND MOUSE. MAKE SURE DOTS AND NUMBERS ARE SHOWING THROUGH SMALL CUT OUT BOX AREAS ON PUMPKIN. CHILD WILL MOVE SMALL MOUSE TO SEE IF ANSWER IS CORRECT.

FINCH FAMILY GAMES © 1994

*REPRODUCE SNOWMAN ONTO HEAVIER CARDSTOCK. COLOR
AND CUT OUT. CUT
OUT SMALL BOX
AREAS.

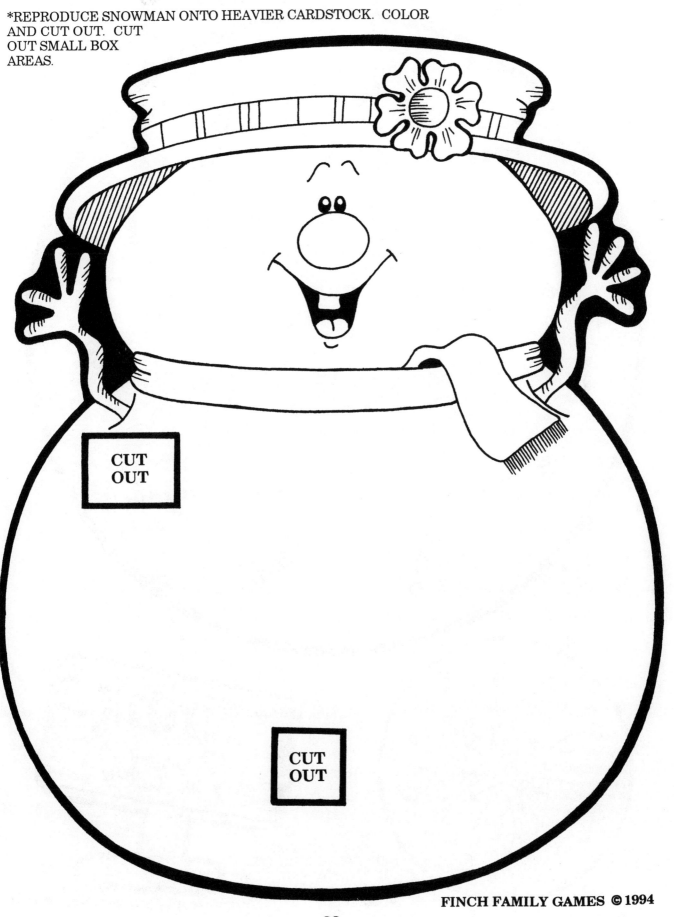

CUT
OUT

CUT
OUT

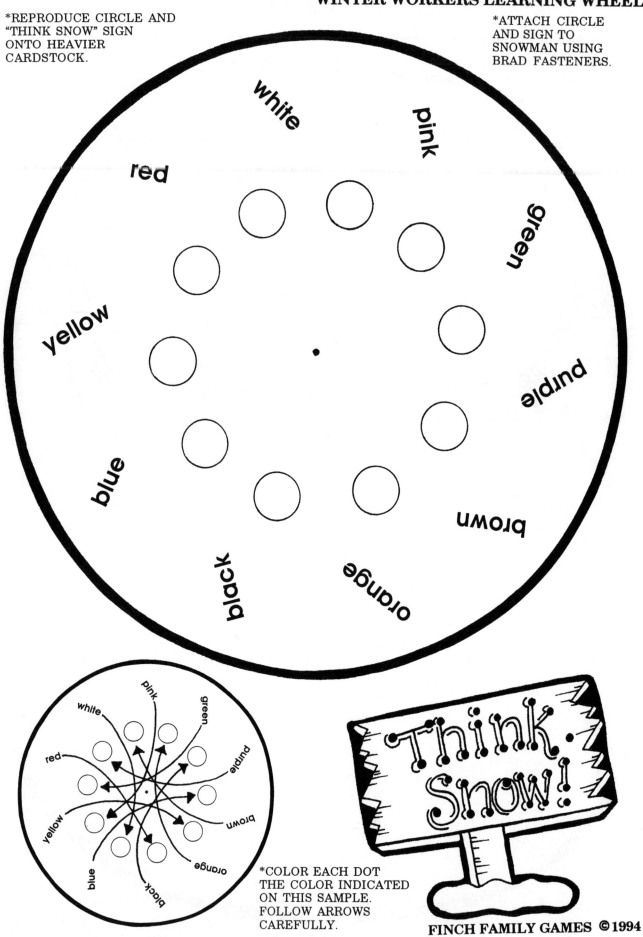

*REPRODUCE CIRCLE AND
"THINK SNOW" SIGN
ONTO HEAVIER
CARDSTOCK.

*ATTACH CIRCLE
AND SIGN TO
SNOWMAN USING
BRAD FASTENERS.

white

pink

red

green

yellow

purple

blue

brown

black

orange

pink

white

green

red

purple

yellow

brown

blue

orange

black

*COLOR EACH DOT
THE COLOR INDICATED
ON THIS SAMPLE.
FOLLOW ARROWS
CAREFULLY.

Think Snow!

FINCH FAMILY GAMES ©1994

*REPRODUCE CLOWN ON HEAVIER
CARDSTOCK. COLOR AND
CUT OUT. CUT OUT
SMALL BOX AREAS.

CUT
OUT

CUT
OUT

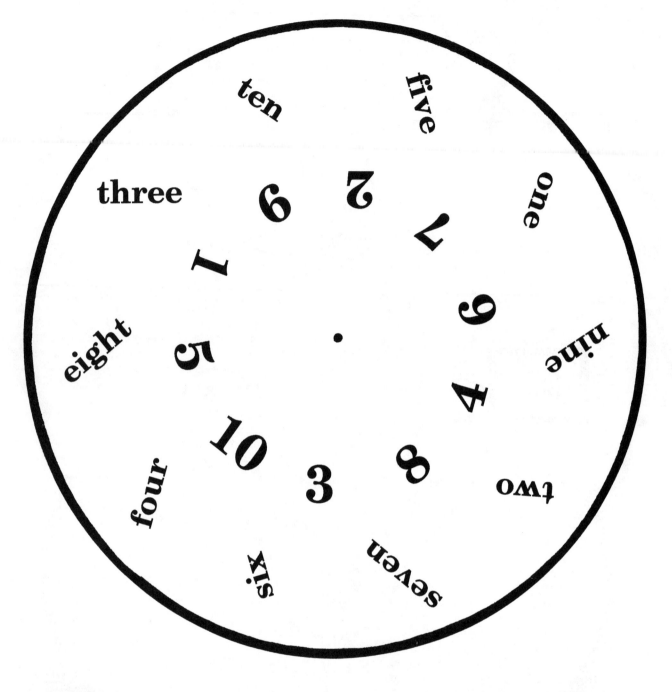

*REPRODUCE CIRCLE AND BANDAID ONTO
HEAVIER CARDSTOCK. COLOR AND CUT
OUT. POKE BRAD FASTENERS THROUGH
BLACK DOTS ON CLOWN, CIRCLE AND
BANDAID. CHILD WILL MOVE BANDAID
WHEN CHECKING ANSWER ON LEARNING
WHEEL.

FINCH FAMILY GAMES © 1994

*COLOR AND CUT OUT EACH
SHAPE PIECE. ASSEMBLE
BY GLUING ALL PIECES
TOGETHER AS SHOWN ON
THE NEXT PAGE OR
ATTACH USING BRAD
FASTENERS (EXCEPT HAT).

*COLOR AND CUT OUT EACH
SHAPE PIECE. ASSEMBLE
AS SHOWN USING GLUE OR
BRAD FASTENERS.

"CLOWN SHAPES"

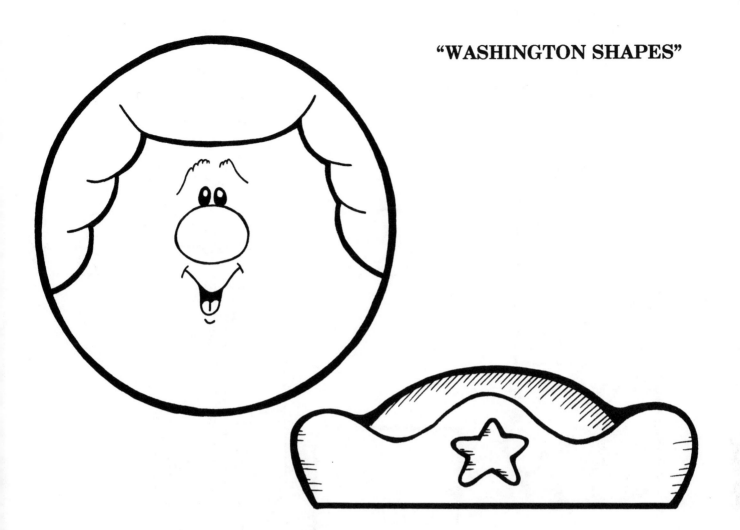

*COLOR AND CUT OUT EACH
SHAPE PIECE. ASSEMBLE BY
GLUING ALL PIECES TOGETHER
AS SHOWN ON THE NEXT
PAGE OR ATTACH USING BRAD
FASTENERS (EXCEPT HAT).

*COLOR AND CUT OUT EACH
SHAPE PIECE. ASSEMBLE
AS SHOWN USING GLUE OR
BRAD FASTENERS.

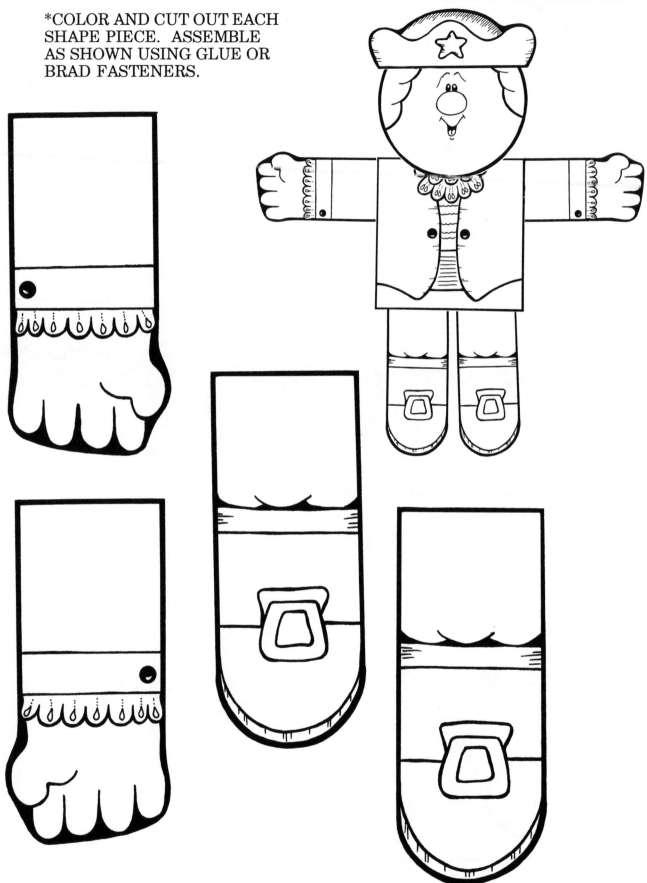

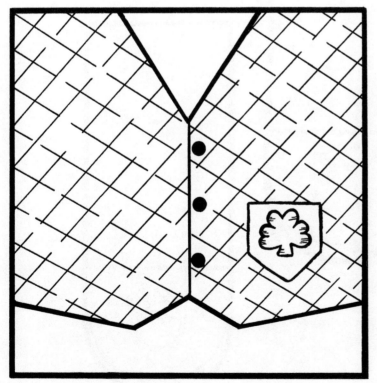

*COLOR AND CUT OUT EACH
SHAPE PIECE. ASSEMBLE BY
GLUING ALL PIECES TOGETHER
AS SHOWN ON THE NEXT
PAGE OR ATTACH USING BRAD
FASTENERS (EXCEPT HAT).

"LEPRECHAUN SHAPES"

*COLOR AND CUT OUT EACH
SHAPE PIECE. ASSEMBLE
AS SHOWN USING GLUE OR
BRAD FASTENERS.

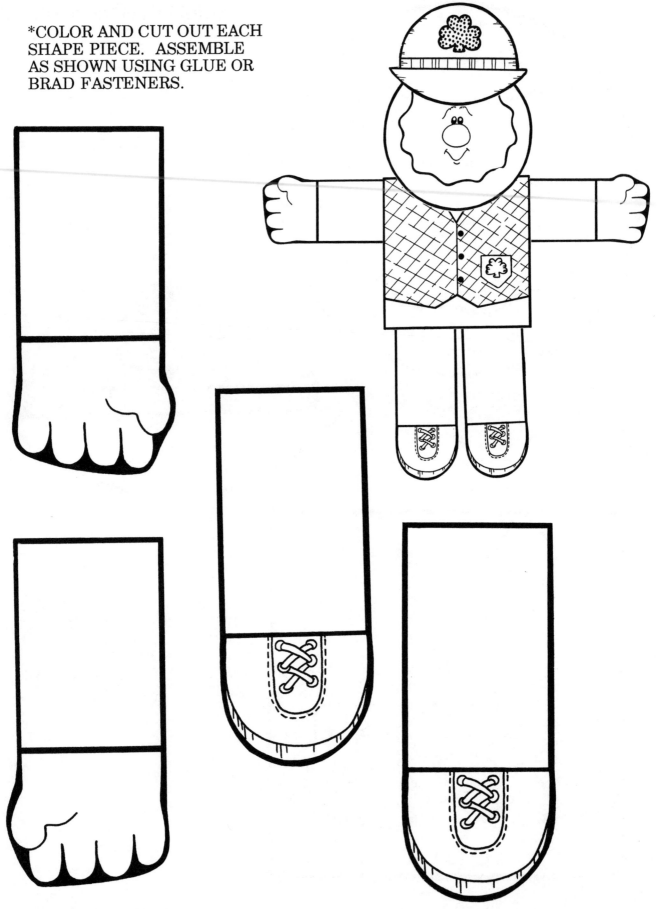

FINCH FAMILY GAMES ©1994

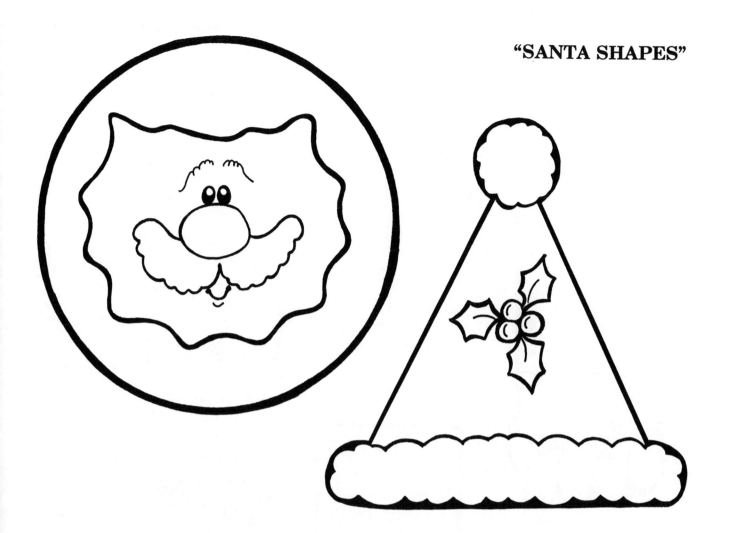

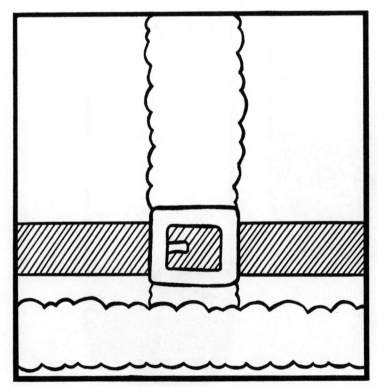

*COLOR AND CUT OUT EACH
SHAPE PIECE. ASSEMBLE BY
GLUING ALL PIECES TOGETHER
AS SHOWN ON THE NEXT
PAGE OR ATTACH USING BRAD
FASTENERS (EXCEPT HAT).

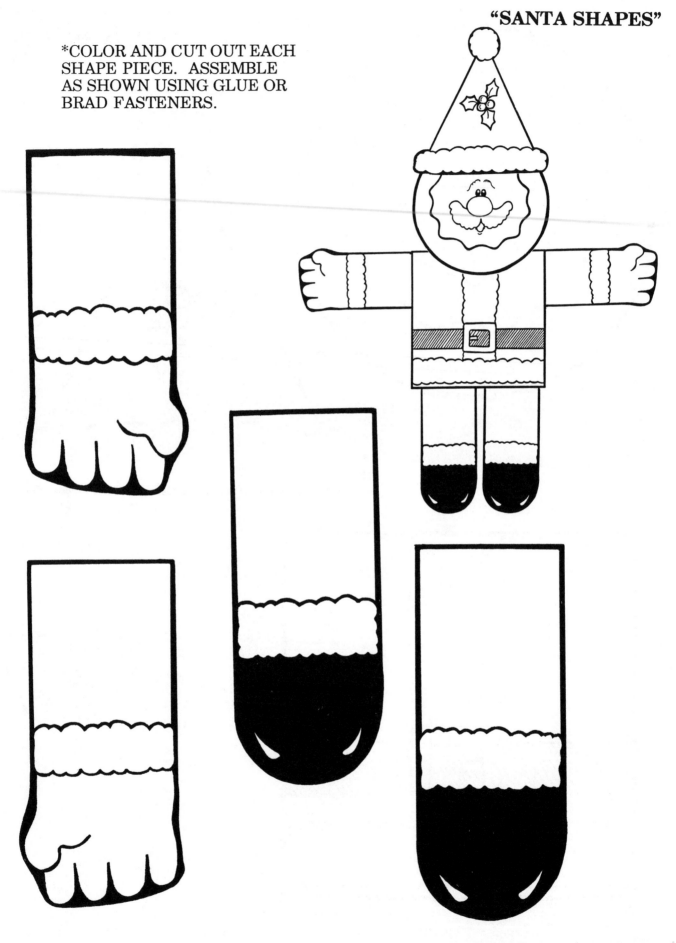

"SANTA SHAPES"

*COLOR AND CUT OUT EACH
SHAPE PIECE. ASSEMBLE
AS SHOWN USING GLUE OR
BRAD FASTENERS.

FINCH FAMILY GAMES © 1994

44

*REPRODUCE HEAD ONTO HEAVIER
CARDSTOCK. CUT OUT EYE AREAS
AND CUT SLITS ALONG SIDE OF
HEAD.

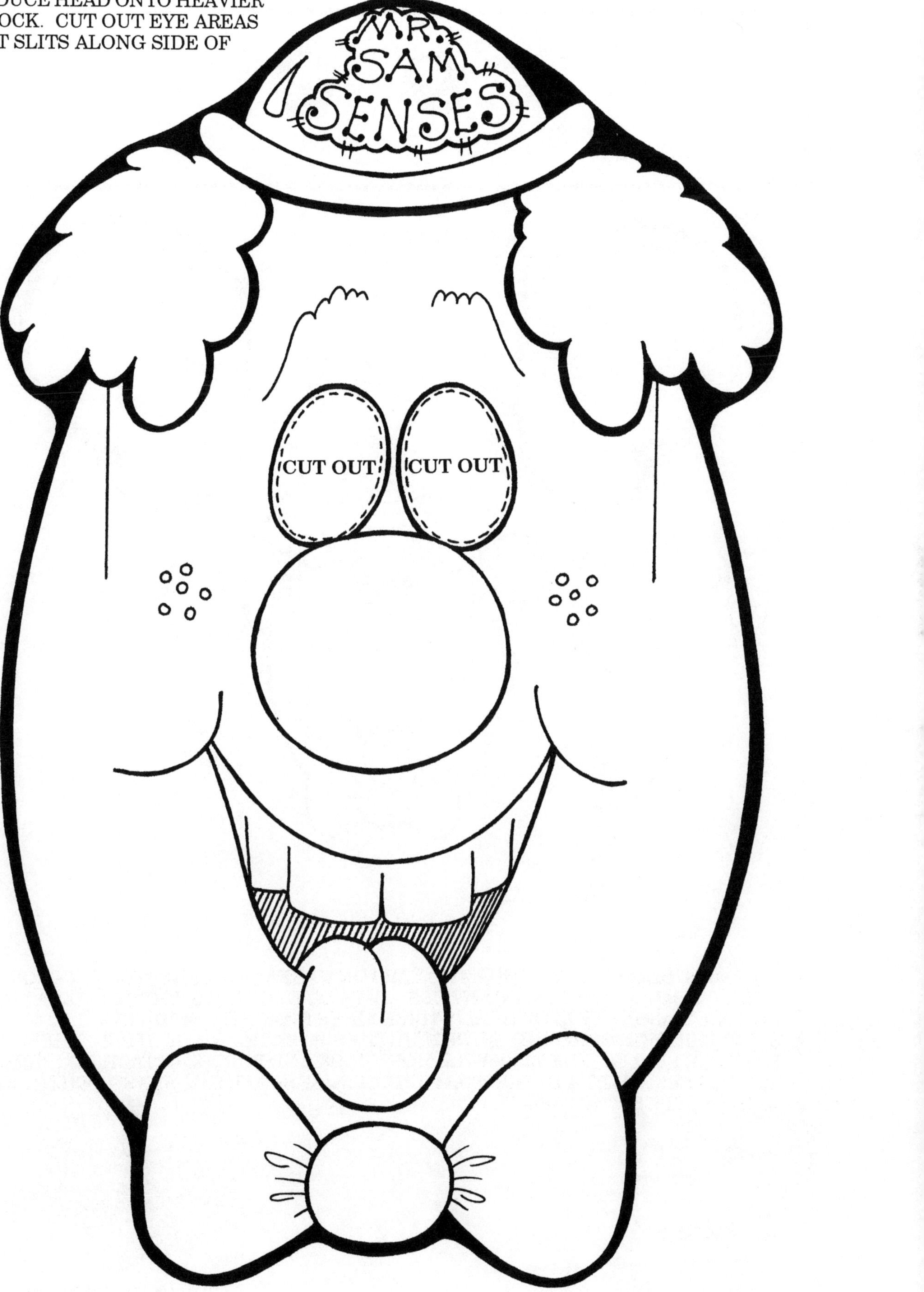

MR. SAM SENSES

CUT OUT   CUT OUT

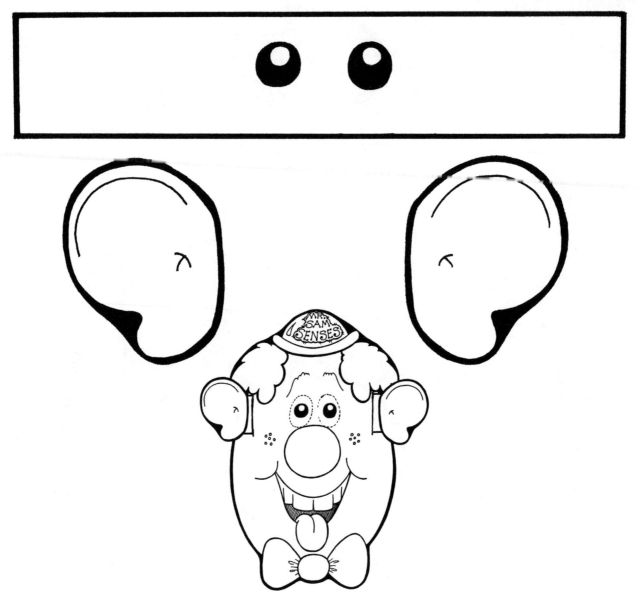

*REPRODUCE HEAD, EYE STRIP AND EARS ONTO HEAVIER CARDSTOCK. COLOR AND CUT OUT ALL PARTS AND PIECES. CUT OUT EYE AREAS WHERE INDICATED. CUT SLITS ALONG SIDE OF HEAD WHERE LINES INDICATE. SLIDE EYE STRIP THROUGH SLITS AND THEN GLUE EARS TO EACH END OF STRIP. WHEN EARS ARE PULLED, THE EYES WILL MOVE BACK AND FORTH. ATTACH FINISHED MR. SAM SENSES TO A DEPRESSOR STICK. FINISHED MR. SAM SENSES WILL LOOK LIKE SAMPLE SHOWN ABOVE.

*REPRODUCE TOP PORTION OF PUPPET ONTO CONSTRUCTION PAPER. COLOR AND CUT OUT. MOUNT ON TOP OF FLAP ON PAPER SACK.

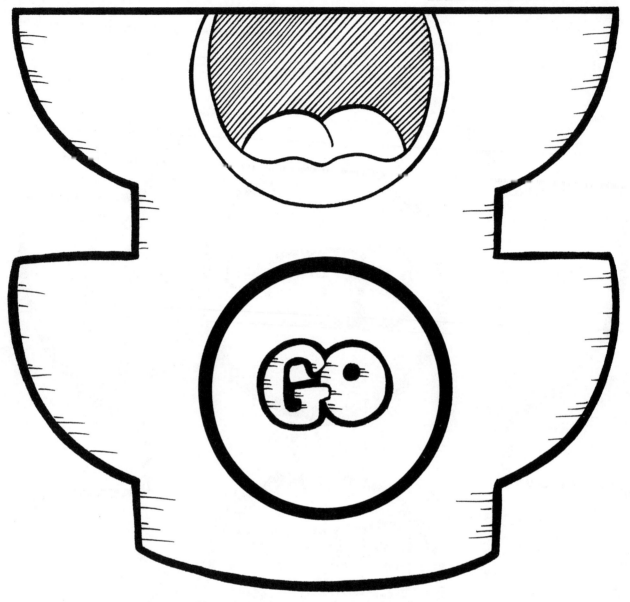

*REPRODUCE BOTTOM PORTION OF PUPPET ONTO CONSTRUCTION PAPER. COLOR AND CUT OUT. MOUNT UNDER FLAP OF PAPER SACK. COMPLETED TRAFFIC LIGHT PUPPET WILL LOOK LIKE SAMPLE SHOWN.

I HAVE TWO FEET, I'M GLAD TO SAY
THAT HELP ME GET AROUND EACH DAY.
THEY WALK AND RUN AND JUMP AND HOP.
SOMETIMES IT'S HARD TO MAKE THEM STOP.
ALTHOUGH MY FEET SURE LOVE TO PLAY,
MY FEET HAVE MANNERS TO OBEY.
THEY WILL NOT KICK WHEN THEY FEEL BAD,
OR STOMP REAL HARD WHEN THEY ARE MAD.
I KNOW MY FEET WILL DO AS THEY SHOULD,
AND THAT WILL MAKE ALL OF ME FEEL GOOD!

*REPRODUCE TWO SHOES FOR
EACH CHILD ONTO HEAVIER
CARDSTOCK. COLOR AND
CUT OUT. CUT ALONG DOTTED
LINE ON HEEL AND CUT OUT
LARGE CIRCLE AREA. PLACE
AROUND ANKLE AND TAPE
CLOSED, IF NEEDED.

CUT OUT

FINCH FAMILY GAMES © 1994

49

*REPRODUCE THE UNDER WATER SCENE ONTO CARDSTOCK OR CONSTRUCTION PAPER. CUT CIRCLE OUT. MOUNT CIRCLE TO INSIDE OF PAPER PLATE. COLOR AND THEN WASH WITH BLUE WATERCOLOR PAINTS THAT ARE WATERED DOWN. TAKE A SECOND PAPER PLATE AND CUT INDENTED CIRCLE SECTION IN CENTER OUT. PLACE CLEAR OR COLORED PLASTIC WRAP ACROSS HOLE AND TAPE INTO POSITION. PUT PAPER PLATES TOGETHER SO THAT UNDER WATER SCENE SHOWS THROUGH PRE-CUT HOLE. COMPLETED PROJECT WILL LOOK LIKE SAMPLE SHOWN.

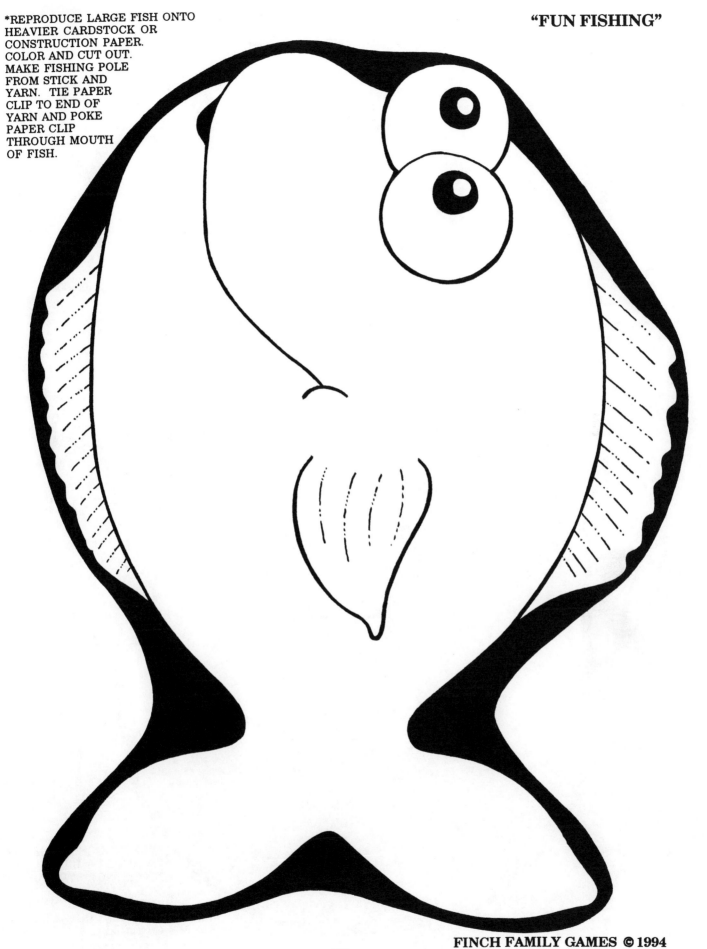

*REPRODUCE LARGE FISH ONTO
HEAVIER CARDSTOCK OR
CONSTRUCTION PAPER.
COLOR AND CUT OUT.
MAKE FISHING POLE
FROM STICK AND
YARN. TIE PAPER
CLIP TO END OF
YARN AND POKE
PAPER CLIP
THROUGH MOUTH
OF FISH.

"FUN FISHING"

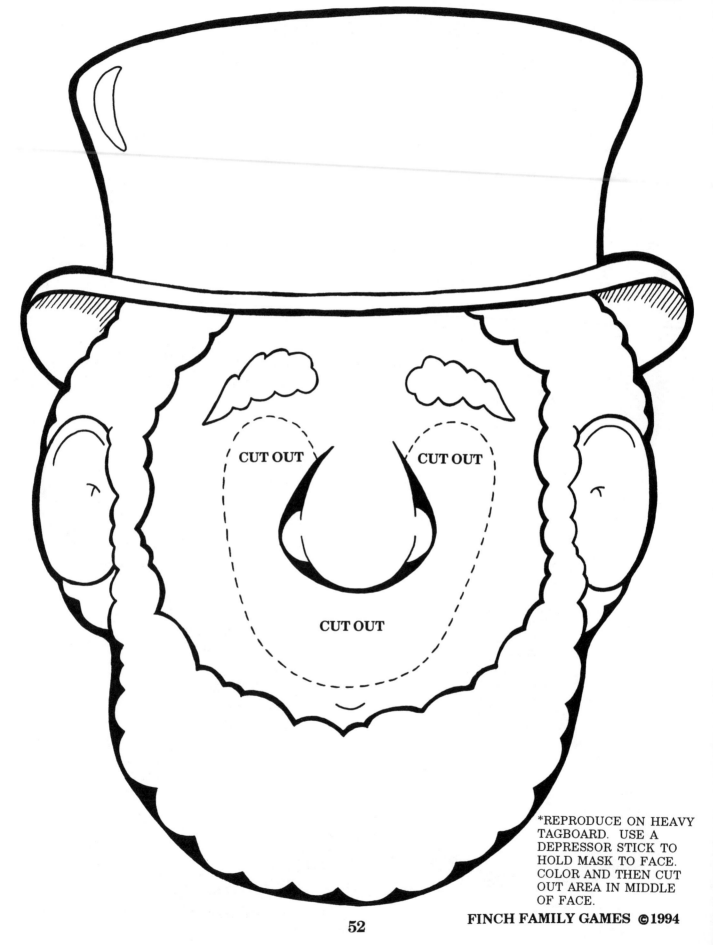

CUT OUT   CUT OUT

CUT OUT

*REPRODUCE ON HEAVY
TAGBOARD. USE A
DEPRESSOR STICK TO
HOLD MASK TO FACE.
COLOR AND THEN CUT
OUT AREA IN MIDDLE
OF FACE.

52   **FINCH FAMILY GAMES ©1994**

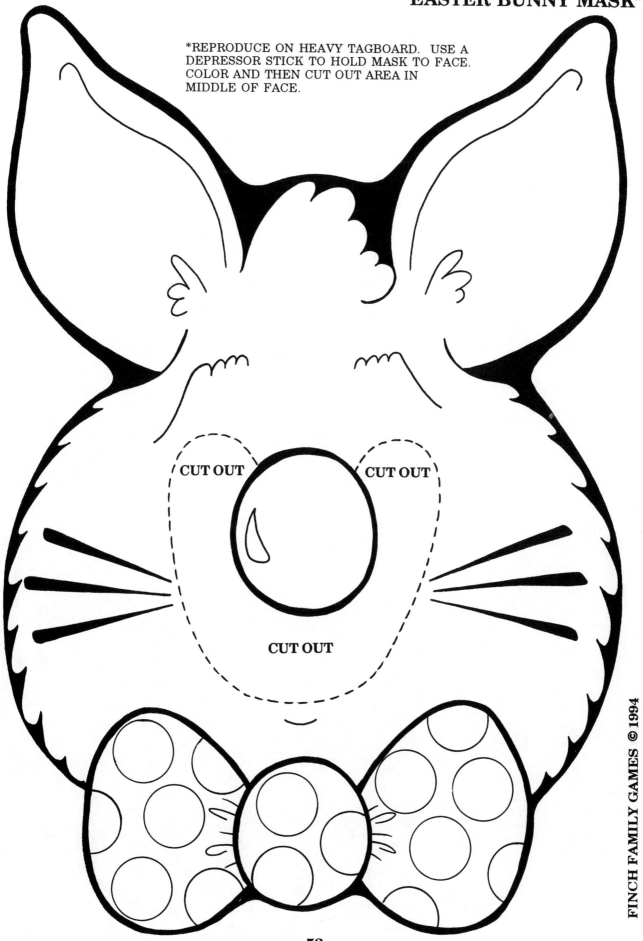

"EASTER BUNNY MASK"

*REPRODUCE ON HEAVY TAGBOARD. USE A DEPRESSOR STICK TO HOLD MASK TO FACE. COLOR AND THEN CUT OUT AREA IN MIDDLE OF FACE.

CUT OUT

CUT OUT

CUT OUT

53

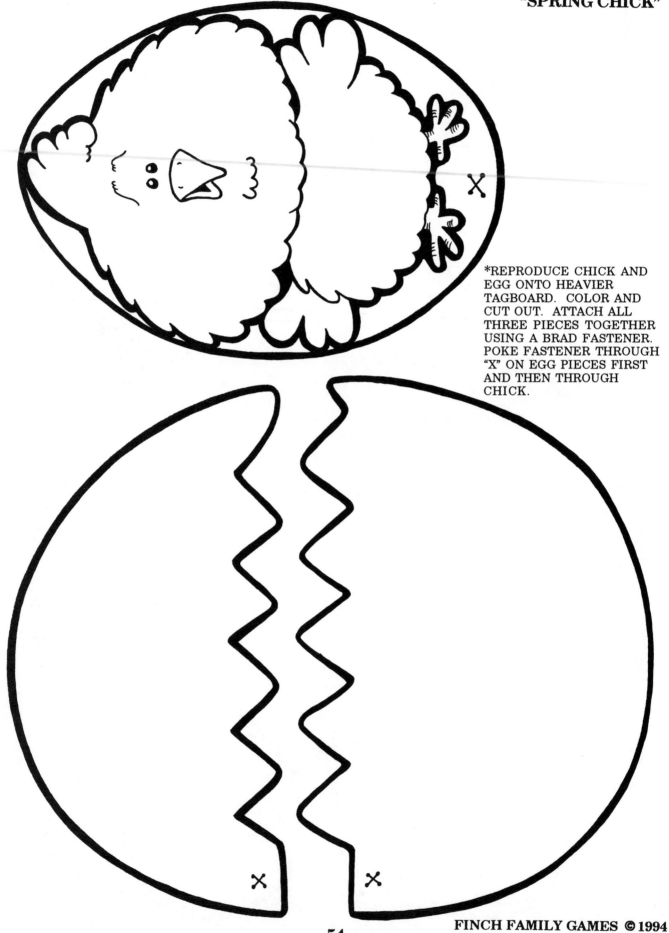

*REPRODUCE CHICK AND
EGG ONTO HEAVIER
TAGBOARD. COLOR AND
CUT OUT. ATTACH ALL
THREE PIECES TOGETHER
USING A BRAD FASTENER.
POKE FASTENER THROUGH
"X" ON EGG PIECES FIRST
AND THEN THROUGH
CHICK.

FINCH FAMILY GAMES © 1994

*REPRODUCE BASKET ONTO
CONSTRUCTION PAPER
COLOR AND CUT OUT. CUT
OUT CENTER OF HANDLE.
PLACE ON ANOTHER
COLOR CONSTRUCTION
PAPER AND TRACE
ANOTHER BASKET.
CUT OUT SECOND
BASKET. HOLDING
TWO BASKETS
TOGETHER, PUNCH
HOLES ALONG EDGES.
SEWING TWO BASKETS
TOGETHER. FILL
WITH EASTER GRASS
OR PAPER EGGS LIKE
THOSE ON FOLLOWING
PAGE.

CUT
OUT

HAPPY EASTER!

FINCH FAMILY GAMES © 1994

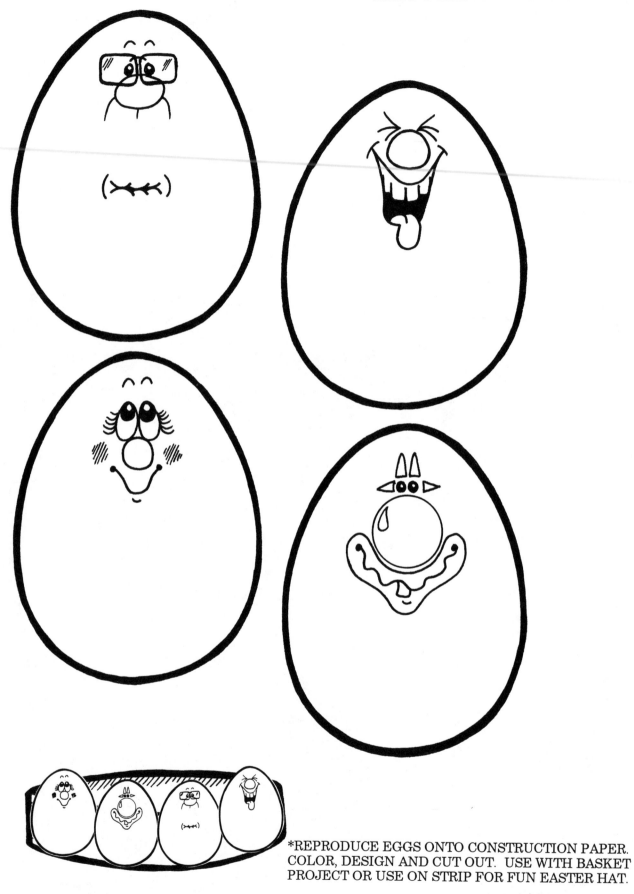

*REPRODUCE EGGS ONTO CONSTRUCTION PAPER.
COLOR, DESIGN AND CUT OUT. USE WITH BASKET
PROJECT OR USE ON STRIP FOR FUN EASTER HAT.

FINCH FAMILY GAMES ©1994

56

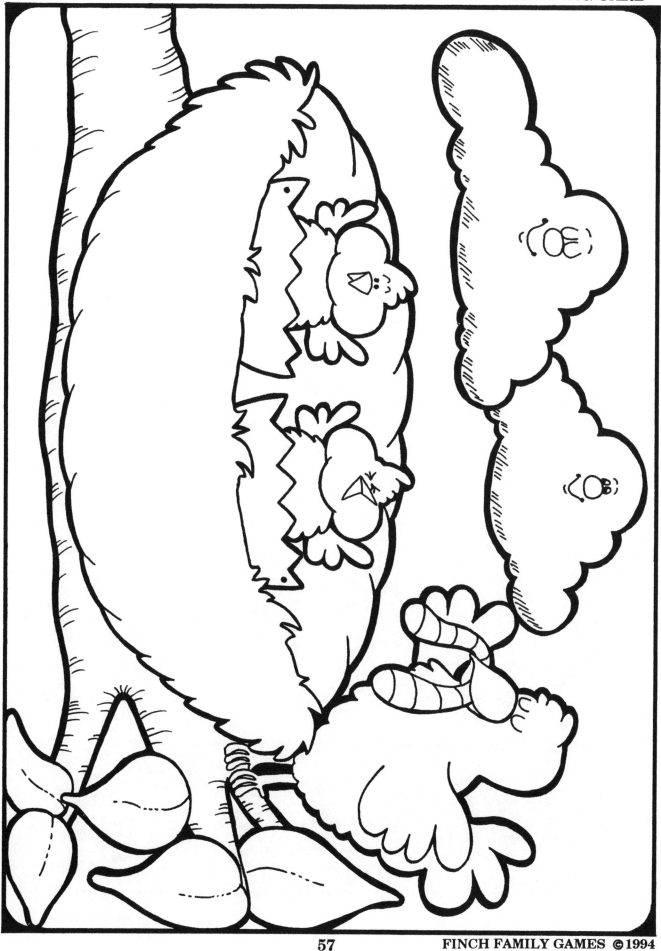

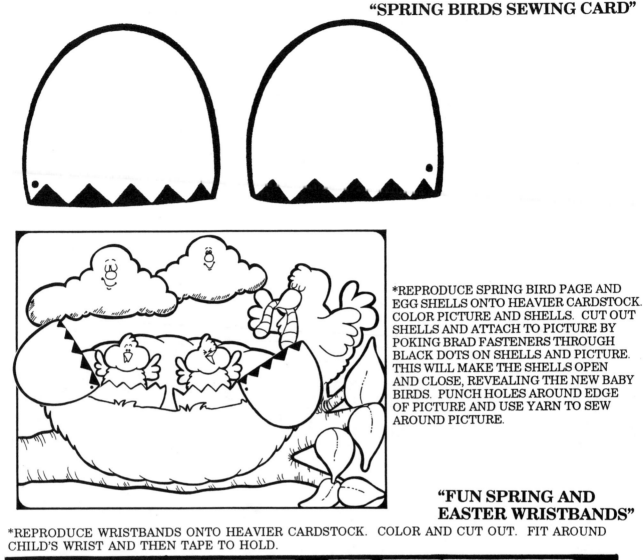

*REPRODUCE SPRING BIRD PAGE AND
EGG SHELLS ONTO HEAVIER CARDSTOCK.
COLOR PICTURE AND SHELLS. CUT OUT
SHELLS AND ATTACH TO PICTURE BY
POKING BRAD FASTENERS THROUGH
BLACK DOTS ON SHELLS AND PICTURE.
THIS WILL MAKE THE SHELLS OPEN
AND CLOSE, REVEALING THE NEW BABY
BIRDS. PUNCH HOLES AROUND EDGE
OF PICTURE AND USE YARN TO SEW
AROUND PICTURE.

**"FUN SPRING AND
EASTER WRISTBANDS"**

*REPRODUCE WRISTBANDS ONTO HEAVIER CARDSTOCK. COLOR AND CUT OUT. FIT AROUND
CHILD'S WRIST AND THEN TAPE TO HOLD.

FINCH FAMILY GAMES ©1994

*REPRODUCE RECIPE BOOK FRONT FOR EACH CHILD. TYPE CHILD'S RECIPE ON CARD.
REPRODUCE RECIPE CARD FOR EACH CHILD IN CLASS. BIND ALONG EDGE OR STAPLE.

A recipe book for a special mom

HAPPY MOTHER'S DAY

Happy
Father's
Day

THIS COUPON CAN BE
USED EVERY DAY OF
THE WEEK....
IT'S WORTH ONE
BIG HUG
AND A KISS ON
THE CHEEK!

*REPRODUCE COUPONS ONTO HEAVIER
CARDSTOCK. COLOR AND CUT OUT.
PUNCH HOLES IN TOP AND TIE BOOKLET
TOGETHER.

PRESENT THIS COUPON
WHEN MY ROOM LOOKS
REAL BAD...
AND I'LL CLEAN IT UP
QUICKLY AND MAKE
BOTH OF US GLAD!!

FINCH FAMILY GAMES © 1994

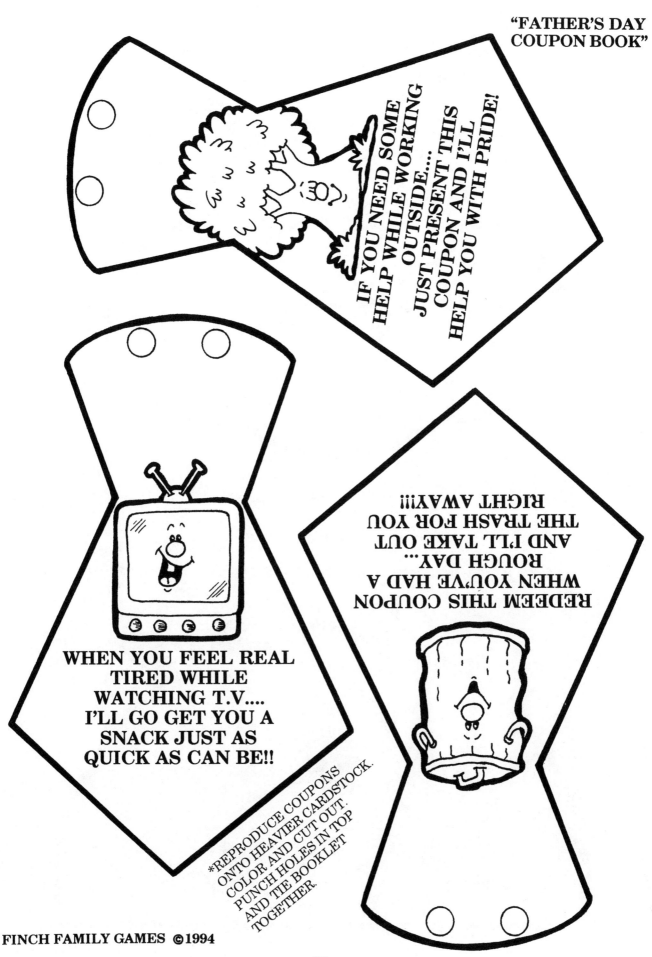

IF YOU NEED SOME
HELP WHILE WORKING
OUTSIDE....
JUST PRESENT THIS
COUPON AND I'LL
HELP YOU WITH PRIDE!

WHEN YOU FEEL REAL
TIRED WHILE
WATCHING T.V....
I'LL GO GET YOU A
SNACK JUST AS
QUICK AS CAN BE!!

REDEEM THIS COUPON
WHEN YOU'VE HAD A
ROUGH DAY....
AND I'LL TAKE OUT
THE TRASH FOR YOU
RIGHT AWAY!!!

*REPRODUCE COUPONS
ONTO HEAVIER CARDSTOCK.
COLOR AND CUT OUT.
PUNCH HOLES IN TOP
AND TIE THE BOOKLET
TOGETHER.

FINCH FAMILY GAMES ©1994

*REPRODUCE HEAD OF BUTTERFLY.
COLOR AND CUT OUT. MOUNT ON TOP OF FLAP OF PAPER SACK.

"CATERPILLAR PUPPET"

*REPRODUCE HEAD OF CATERPILLAR. COLOR AND CUT OUT. MOUNT ON TOP OF FLAP
OF PAPER SACK.

FINCH FAMILY GAMES ©1994

"BUTTERFLY PUPPET"

*REPRODUCE BODY OF CATERPILLAR. COLOR AND CUT OUT. MOUNT UNDER FLAP OF PAPER SACK.

I'M A LITTLE CATERPILLAR
    JUST CRAWLING ALL AROUND.
LOOKING FOR SOMETHING TO EAT,
    I HARDLY MAKE A SOUND.
BUT I WILL KEEP ON GROWING
    FOR I AM GOING TO TRY,
TO CHANGE MY FUZZY BODY
    INTO A BUTTERFLY!!

HOW TO MAKE: COLOR, CUT OUT AND MOUNT CIRCLE PARTS TO CATERPILLAR SILHOUETTE ON NEXT PAGE. THIS CAN BE USED AS A FUN ART ACTIVITY BY REPRODUCING THE FOLLOWING PAGE ONTO A HEAVIER CARDSTOCK. THE CHILD CAN PAINT OR COLOR THIS PAGE AND IF YOU WANT, PUNCH HOLES ALONG THE OUTSIDE EDGES AND MAKE THIS INTO A SEWING CARD ACTIVITY.

VARIATION: THIS ACTIVITY CAN ALSO BE USED AS AN INCENTIVE CHART BY MAKING ONE FOR EACH CHILD. HAVE CHILD COLOR THE PAGE AND THE INDIVIDUAL CIRCLES. PLACE THE CIRCLES IN AN ENVELOPE WITH THAT CHILD'S NAME ON IT. EACH TIME THE CHILD DOES SOMETHING POSITIVE (GOOD TEST SCORE, COMPLETED HOMEWORK, KINDNESS TO OTHERS, ETC.), HAVE HIM PUT A CATERPILLAR PIECE ON HIS CHART. WHEN THE CATERPILLAR IS COMPLETED, DO SOMETHING FUN OR GIVE THE CHILD A SPECIAL REWARD.

THE CATERPILLAR SO FUZZY
AND SWEET......
IS ALWAYS LOOKING FOR
SOMETHING TO EAT!

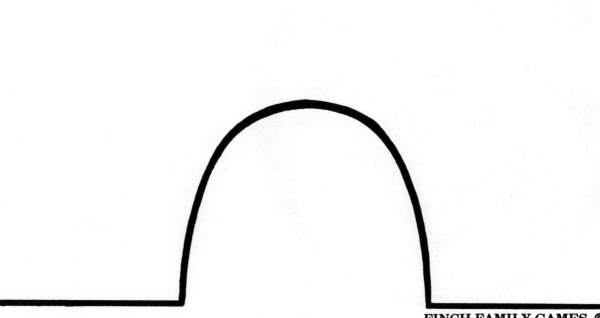

"ANIMALS ON PARADE!"

*REPRODUCE ANIMAL BODY
PATTERN. CUT OUT AND
FOLD ALONG DOTTED LINE.
DESIGN ANIMAL USING OWN
CREATIVITY DEPENDING ON
WHICH ANIMAL IT IS.

"ANIMALS ON PARADE!"

*REPRODUCE ANIMAL HEADS ONTO CONSTRUCTION PAPER. COLOR AND CUT OUT. MOUNT TO BODY PORTION OF ANIMAL. DESIGN BODY USING OWN CREATIVITY. (BODY PATTERN IS ON PREVIOUS PAGE.) SAMPLE OF ANIMAL STANDING UP IS SHOWN.

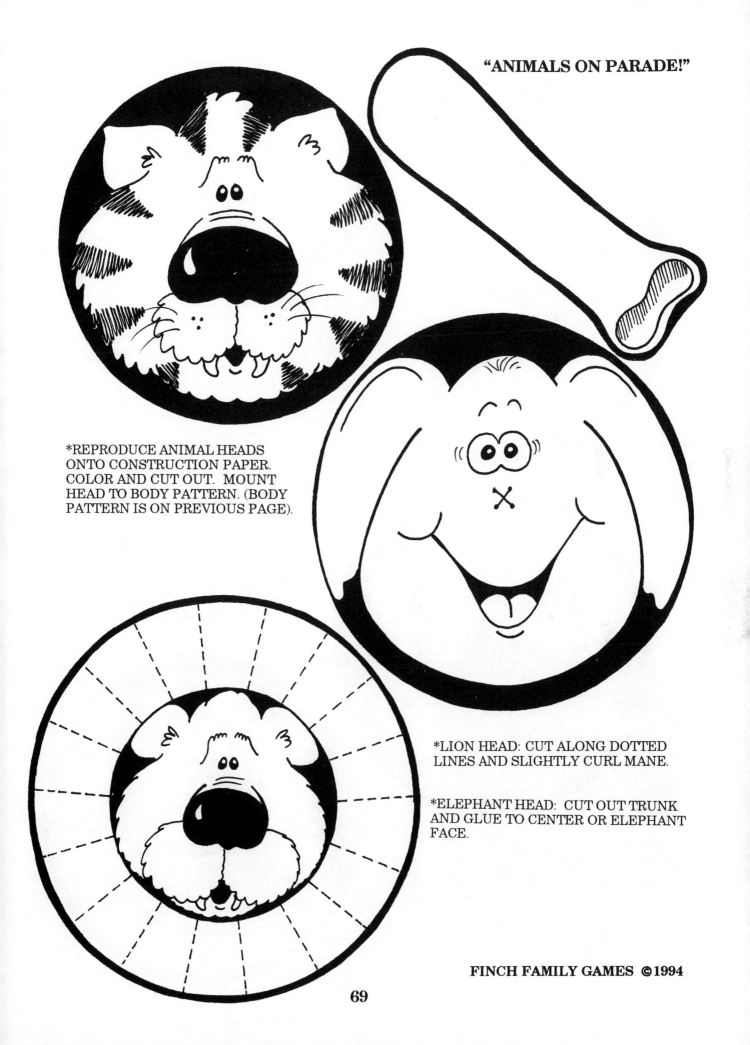

"ANIMALS ON PARADE!"

*REPRODUCE ANIMAL HEADS
ONTO CONSTRUCTION PAPER.
COLOR AND CUT OUT. MOUNT
HEAD TO BODY PATTERN. (BODY
PATTERN IS ON PREVIOUS PAGE).

*LION HEAD: CUT ALONG DOTTED
LINES AND SLIGHTLY CURL MANE.

*ELEPHANT HEAD: CUT OUT TRUNK
AND GLUE TO CENTER OR ELEPHANT
FACE.

FINCH FAMILY GAMES ©1994

69

*REPRODUCE ANIMAL HEADS
ONTO CONSTRUCTION PAPER.
COLOR AND CUT OUT. MOUNT
HEAD TO BODY PATTERN. (BODY
PATTERN IS ON PREVIOUS PAGE).

*COW: CUT OUT UTTER AND
MOUNT TO BACK LEGS OF
BODY PATTERN.

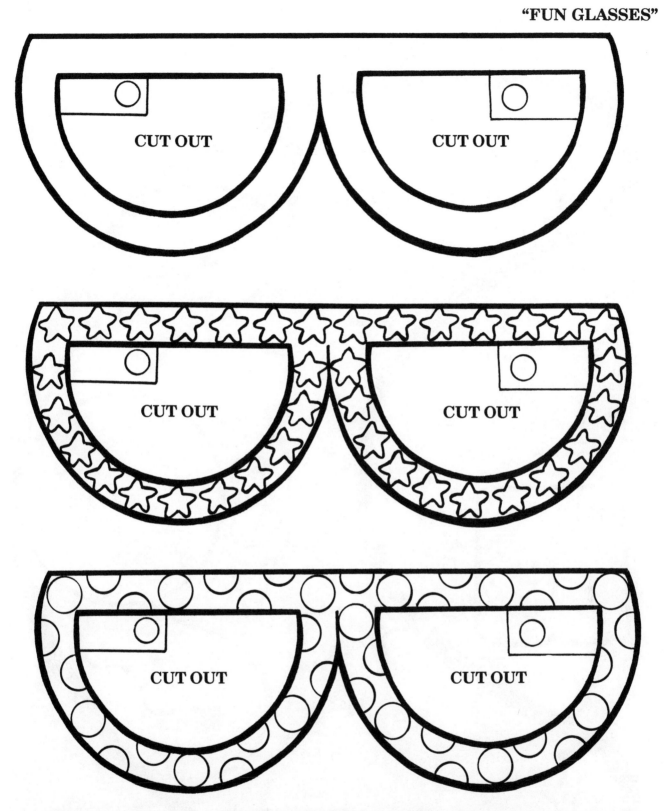

*REPRODUCE THESE GLASSES ONTO HEAVIER CARDSTOCK OR TAGBOARD. COLOR AND DESIGN GLASSES. CUT OUT AREA INSIDE GLASSES. CUT OUT SMALL TAB INSIDE GLASSES AND FOLD BACK. PUNCH HOLE IN TAB. TIE YARN OR ELASTIC TO HOLE TO HOLD GLASSES TO CHILD'S HEAD. TAPE COLORED PLASTIC WRAP TO GLASS AREA OF GLASSES FOR A FUN VISUAL EFFECT.

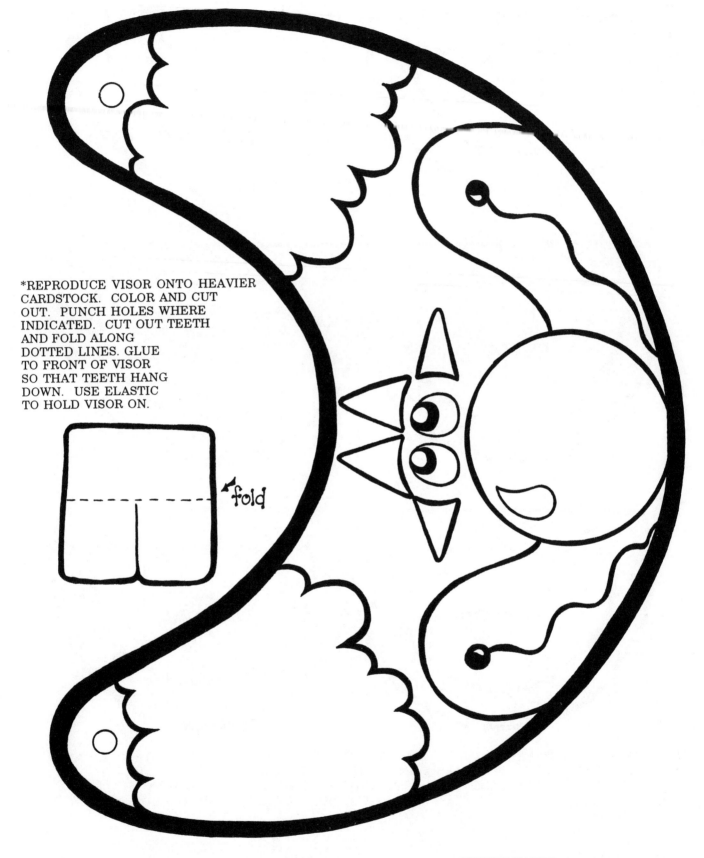

*REPRODUCE VISOR ONTO HEAVIER
CARDSTOCK. COLOR AND CUT
OUT. PUNCH HOLES WHERE
INDICATED. CUT OUT TEETH
AND FOLD ALONG
DOTTED LINES. GLUE
TO FRONT OF VISOR
SO THAT TEETH HANG
DOWN. USE ELASTIC
TO HOLD VISOR ON.

fold

FINCH FAMILY GAMES © 1994

72

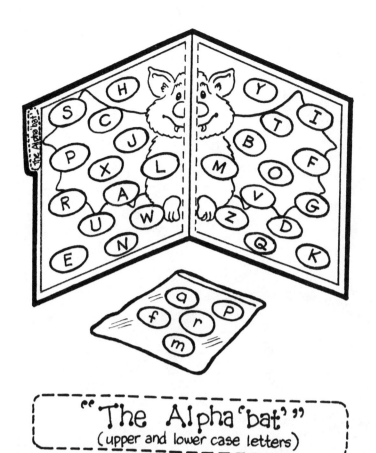

"THE ALPHABAT"

GAME: THE ALPHA"BAT"!

SKILL: UPPER AND LOWER CASE LETTER RECOGNITION

GAME INCLUDES: TWO LARGE PAGES THAT FORM A BAT AND 26 INDIVIDUAL OVALS WITH LETTERS

HOW TO MAKE:
1. COLOR, CUT OUT AND MOUNT TWO LARGE PAGES THAT FORM A BAT ONTO THE INSIDE OF THE FOLDER.
2. COLOR, CUT OUT AND MOUNT INDIVIDUAL OVALS ONTO HEAVIER CARDSTOCK. LAMINATE FOR DURABILITY.
3. CUT OUT GAME LABEL AND MOUNT ON FILE FOLDER TAB.
4. COLOR, CUT OUT AND MOUNT GAME TITLE ON FRONT OF FOLDER.
5. FOR DURABILITY, LAMINATE ENTIRE FOLDER. USE "STICKY-BACK" VELCRO TO HOLD INDIVIDUAL OVALS TO FOLDER WHEN PLAYING.

"The Alpha "bat""
(upper and lower case letters)

*MOUNT ON FILE FOLDER TAB.

*MOUNT ON FRONT OF FOLDER.

FINCH FAMILY GAMES © 1994

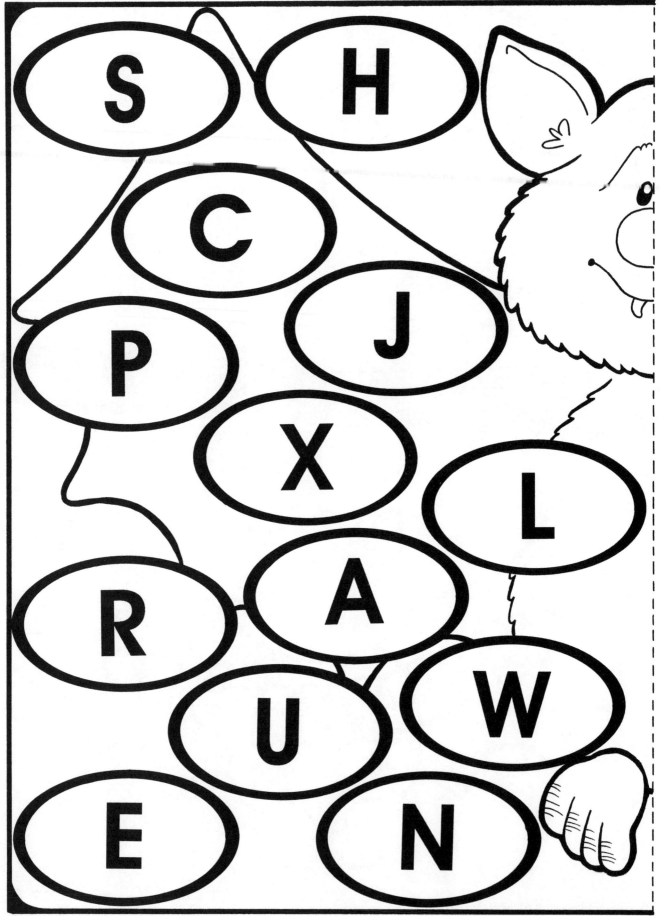

"THE ALPHABAT"

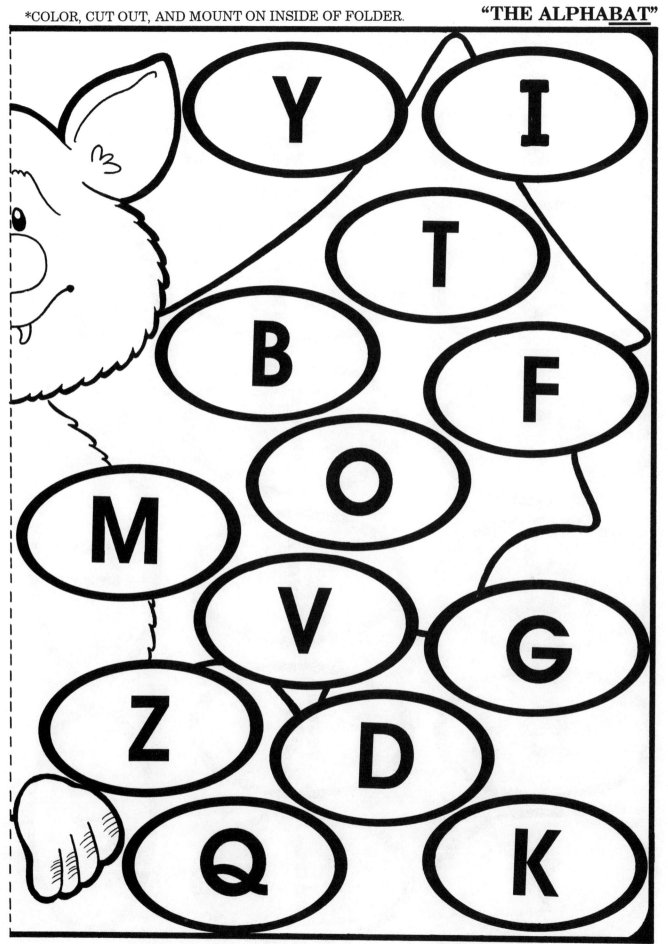

FINCH FAMILY GAMES ©1994

"THE ALPHA<u>BAT</u>"

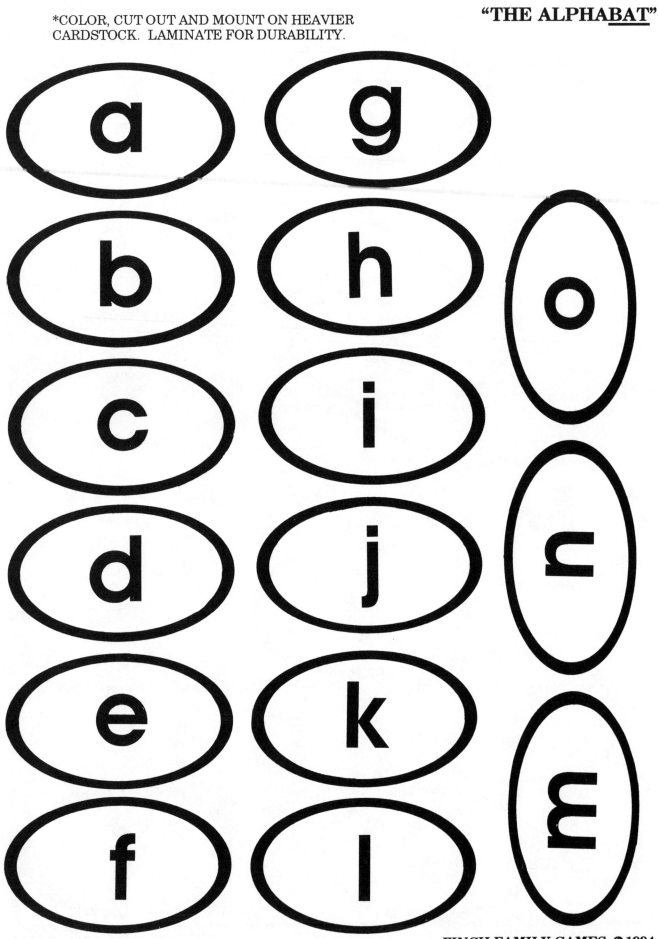

*COLOR, CUT OUT AND MOUNT ON HEAVIER
CARDSTOCK. LAMINATE FOR DURABILITY.

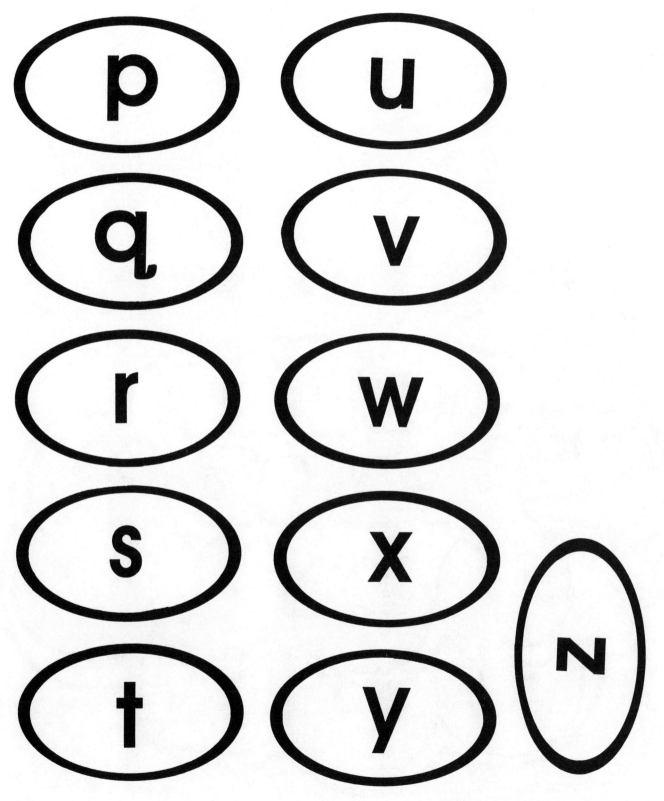

77   FINCH FAMILY GAMES ©1994

"TULIP TIME"

GAME: TULIP TIME

SKILL: COLORS AND COLOR WORDS

GAME INCLUDES: 10 TULIP TOPS AND 10 STEMS AND LEAVES

HOW TO MAKE:
1. COLOR, CUT OUT AND MOUNT STEMS AND LEAVES ONTO INSIDE OF FOLDER. (IF YOU CHOOSE TO MAKE THIS GAME EASY, COLOR THE STEMS EACH THE COLOR THAT IS WRITTEN ON THEM. FOR OLDER CHILDREN, COLOR ALL THE STEMS GREEN AND THEY WILL NEED TO READ THE COLOR WORD INORDER TO PUT THE CORRECT TULIP TOP ON.)
2. COLOR EACH TULIP TOP THE COLOR INDICATED, CUT OUT AND MOUNT ONTO A HEAVIER CARDSTOCK. LAMINATE FOR DURABILITY AND USE "STICKY-BACK" VELCRO TO HOLD TULIP TOPS TO FOLDER WHEN PLAYING.
3. CUT OUT GAME LABEL AND MOUNT ON FILE FOLDER TAB.
4. COLOR, CUT OUT AND MOUNT GAME TITLE ON FRONT OF FOLDER.
5. FOR DURABILITY, LAMINATE ENTIRE FOLDER.

"Tulip Time"
(colors and color words)

*MOUNT ON FILE FOLDER TAB.

*COLOR, CUT OUT AND MOUNT ON FRONT OF FOLDER.

FINCH FAMILY GAMES © 1994

78

*COLOR, CUT OUT, AND MOUNT STEMS AND LEAVES ON INSIDE OF FOLDER. COLOR, CUT OUT AND MOUNT TULIP TOPS ONTO HEAVIER CARDSTOCK. LAMINATE FOR DURABILITY. USE "STICKY-BACK" VELCRO TO HOLD TULIP TOPS TO FOLDER WHEN PLAYING.

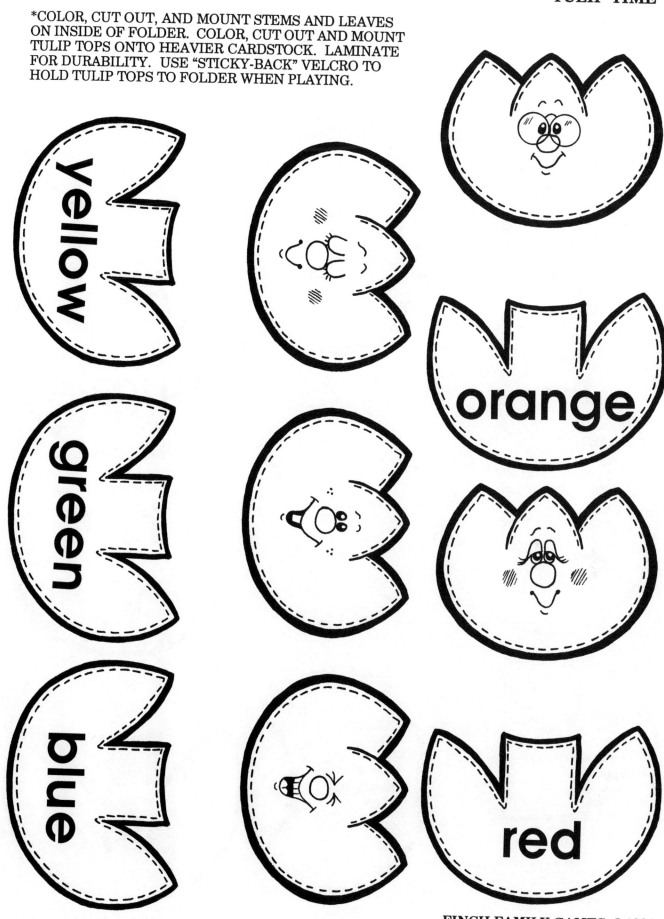

*COLOR, CUT OUT, AND MOUNT STEMS AND LEAVES ON INSIDE OF FOLDER. COLOR, CUT OUT AND MOUNT TULIP TOPS ONTO HEAVIER CARDSTOCK. LAMINATE FOR DURABILITY. USE "STICKY-BACK" VELCRO TO HOLD TULIP TOPS TO FOLDER WHEN PLAYING.

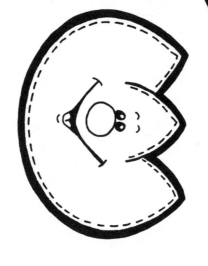

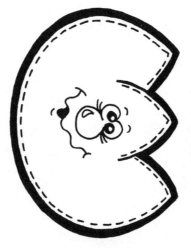

brown

black

white

purple

pink

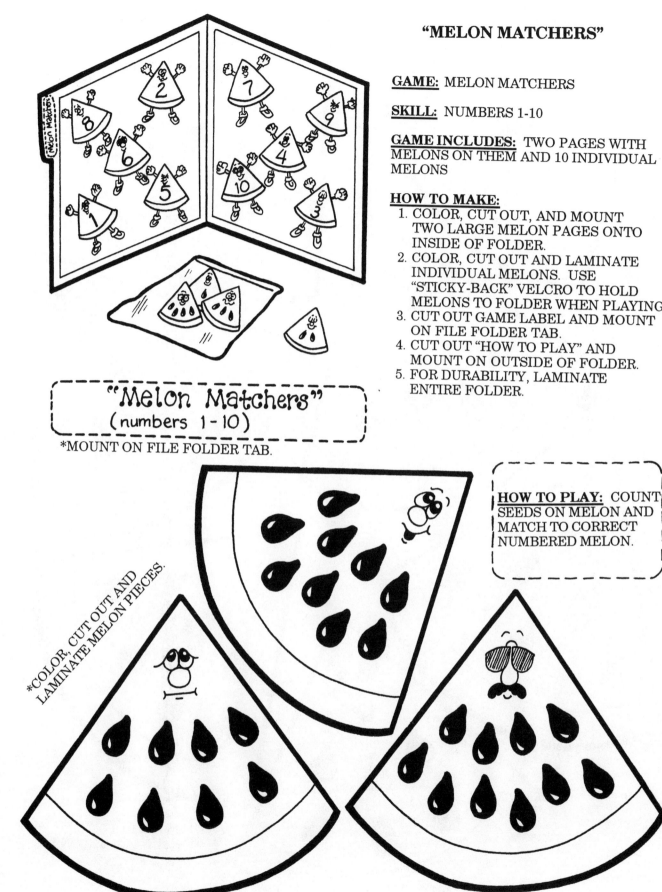

"MELON MATCHERS"

GAME: MELON MATCHERS

SKILL: NUMBERS 1-10

GAME INCLUDES: TWO PAGES WITH MELONS ON THEM AND 10 INDIVIDUAL MELONS

HOW TO MAKE:
1. COLOR, CUT OUT, AND MOUNT TWO LARGE MELON PAGES ONTO INSIDE OF FOLDER.
2. COLOR, CUT OUT AND LAMINATE INDIVIDUAL MELONS. USE "STICKY-BACK" VELCRO TO HOLD MELONS TO FOLDER WHEN PLAYING.
3. CUT OUT GAME LABEL AND MOUNT ON FILE FOLDER TAB.
4. CUT OUT "HOW TO PLAY" AND MOUNT ON OUTSIDE OF FOLDER.
5. FOR DURABILITY, LAMINATE ENTIRE FOLDER.

"Melon Matchers"
(numbers 1-10)
*MOUNT ON FILE FOLDER TAB.

*COLOR, CUT OUT AND LAMINATE MELON PIECES.

HOW TO PLAY: COUNT SEEDS ON MELON AND MATCH TO CORRECT NUMBERED MELON.

"MELON MATCHERS"

*COLOR, CUT OUT
AND LAMINATE MELON PIECES.

FINCH FAMILY GAMES © 1994

82

*MOUNT ON FILE FOLDER TAB.

"Outer Space Face"
(visual discrimination)

HOW TO PLAY: PICK A CARD AND
CREATE THE SAME FACE YOU SEE.

"OUTER SPACE FACE"

GAME: OUTER SPACE FACE

SKILL: VISUAL DISCRIMINATION

GAME INCLUDES: ONE LARGE PAGE WITH
OUTER SPACE HEAD, 12 FACE CARDS,
20 FACE PIECES, ONE CARD HOLDER
AND ONE FACE PIECES HOLDER

HOW TO MAKE:
1. COLOR, CUT OUT, AND MOUNT PAGE
WITH OUTER SPACE HEAD ONTO INSIDE
OF FOLDER.
2. MOUNT CARD HOLDER AND FACE PIECES
HOLDER ONTO INSIDE OF FOLDER BY
GLUING ALONG SIDE AND BOTTOM EDGES
ONLY. THIS WILL FORM A POCKET.
3. COLOR, CUT OUT, AND MOUNT FACE
PIECES ON TAGBOARD.
4. COLOR, CUT OUT, AND MOUNT FACE
CARDS ON TAGBOARD.
5. CUT OUT GAME LABEL AND MOUNT
ON FILE FOLDER TAB.
6. CUT OUT "HOW TO PLAY" AND MOUNT
ON OUTSIDE OF FOLDER.
7. FOR DURABILITY, LAMINATE FOLDER
AND ALL GAME PIECES.

*COLOR, CUT OUT, AND MOUNT ON TAGBOARD.
LAMINATE FOR DURABILITY.

FINCH FAMILY GAMES © 1994

*COLOR, CUT OUT, AND MOUNT ON
TAGBOARD. LAMINATE FOR
DURABILITY.

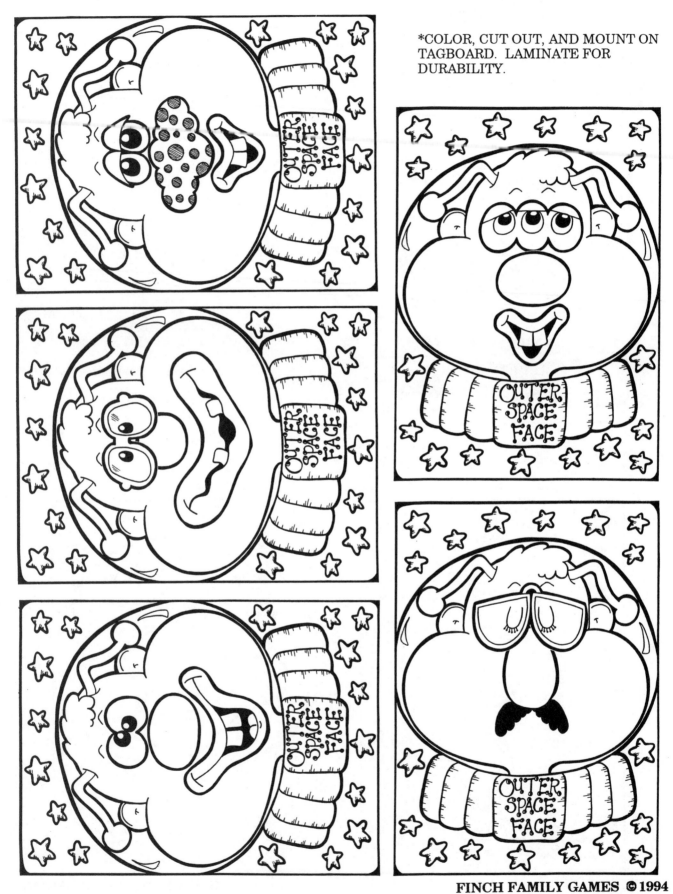

FINCH FAMILY GAMES © 1994

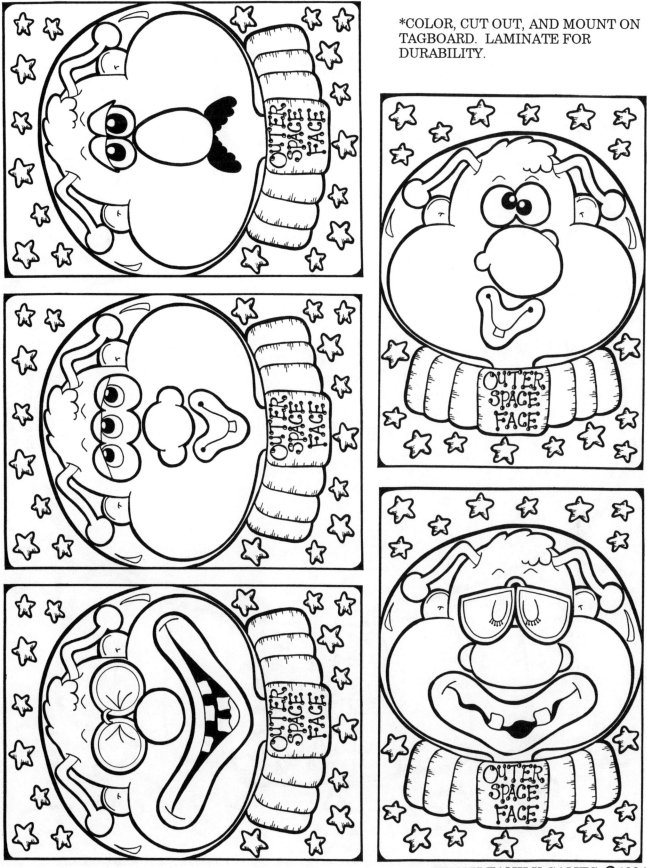

*COLOR, CUT OUT, AND MOUNT ON TAGBOARD. LAMINATE FOR DURABILITY.

*COLOR, CUT OUT, AND MOUNT ON INSIDE OF FOLDER. USE "STICKY-BACK" VELCRO TO HOLD FACE PIECES TO HEAD.

"OUTER SPACE FACE"

FINCH FAMILY GAMES ©1994

*COLOR, CUT OUT, AND MOUNT ON
TAGBOARD. LAMINATE FOR DURABILITY.
USE "STICKY-BACK" VELCRO TO HOLD
PIECES TO FOLDER WHEN PLAYING.

FINCH FAMILY GAMES © 1994

*COLOR, CUT OUT, AND MOUNT ON
TAGBOARD. LAMINATE FOR DURABILITY.
USE "STICKY-BACK" VELCRO TO HOLD
PIECES TO FOLDER WHEN PLAYING.

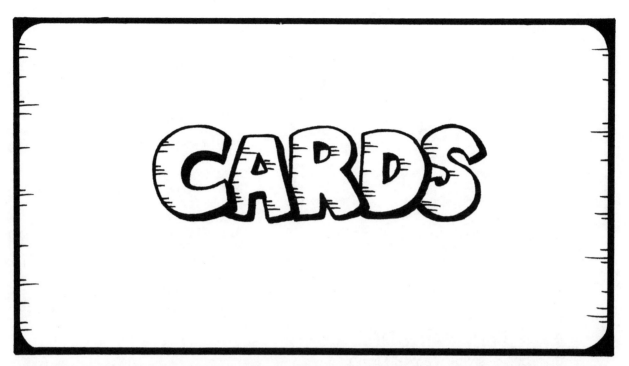

*COLOR, CUT OUT, AND MOUNT CARD HOLDER AND FACE PIECES HOLDER ONTO HEAVIER
TAGBOARD. GLUE TO INSIDE OF FOLDER BY GLUING ALONG SIDE AND BOTTOM EDGES ONLY.
THIS WILL FORM A POCKET HOLDER FOR CARDS AND GAME PIECES. LAMINATE ENTIRE
FOLDER AND THEN USE A SHARP EDGE TO BREAK SEAL AT THE TOP OF EACH POCKET
HOLDER.

"SILLY SHAPES"

GAME: SILLY SHAPES

SKILL: BASIC SHAPE RECOGNITION

GAME INCLUDES: TWO LARGE PAGES WITH 12 DIFFERENT SHAPE CHARACTERS AND 12 INDIVIDUAL SHAPES THAT MATCH.

HOW TO MAKE:
1. COLOR, CUT OUT AND MOUNT TWO LARGE SHAPE PAGES ONTO INSIDE OF FOLDER.
2. COLOR, CUT OUT AND MOUNT INDIVIDUAL SHAPES ONTO HEAVIER CARDSTOCK. LAMINATE FOR DURABILITY.
3. CUT OUT GAME LABEL AND MOUNT ON FILE FOLDER TAB.
4. FOR DURABILITY, LAMINATE ENTIRE FOLDER.
5. USE "STICKY-BACK" VELCRO TO HOLD INDIVIDUAL SHAPES TO FOLDER WHEN PLAYING.

"Silly Shapes"
(basic shape recognition)

*MOUNT ON FILE FOLDER TAB.

*COLOR, CUT OUT AND MOUNT ONTO HEAVIER CARDSTOCK. LAMINATE FOR DURABILITY.

*USE "STICKY-BACK" VELCRO TO HOLD SHAPES TO FOLDER WHEN PLAYING.

FINCH FAMILY GAMES ©1994

*COLOR, CUT OUT AND MOUNT ONTO
HEAVIER CARDSTOCK. LAMINATE
FOR DURABILITY. USE "STICKY-BACK"
VELCRO TO HOLD SHAPES TO FOLDER
WHEN PLAYING.

FINCH FAMILY GAMES ©1994

"SILLY SHAPES"

FINCH FAMILY GAMES ©1994

"SILLY SHAPES"

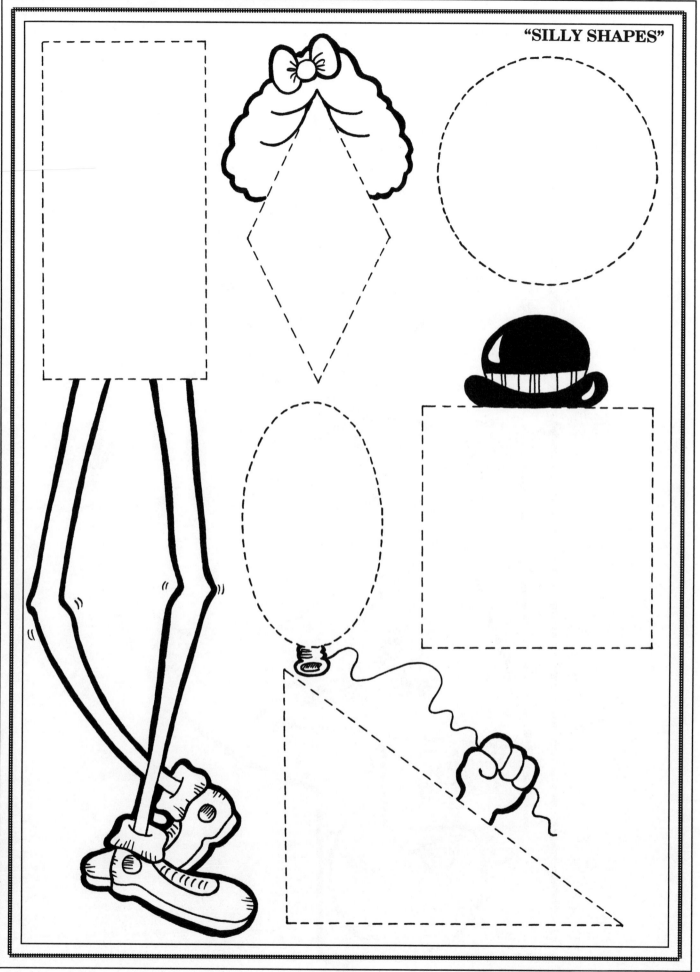

FINCH FAMILY GAMES © 1994

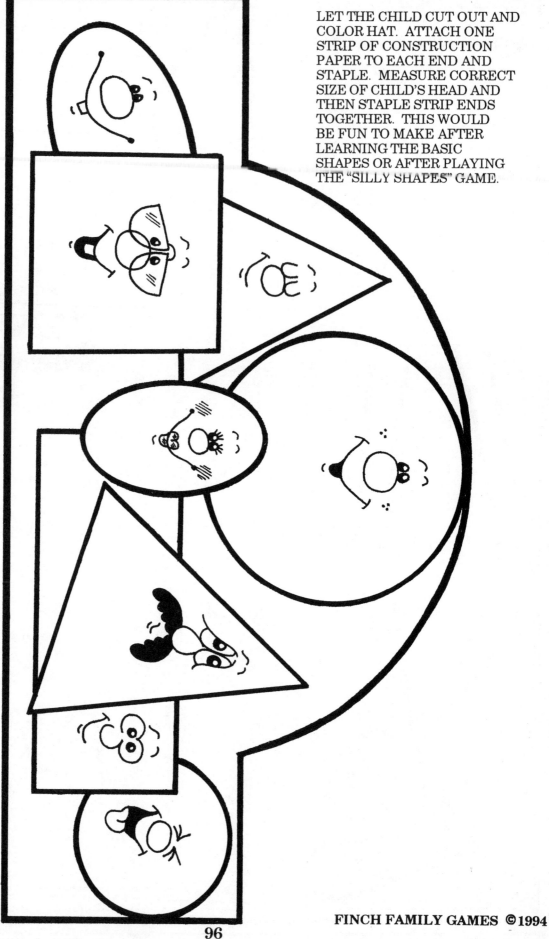

"SUPER SHAPES HAT"

LET THE CHILD CUT OUT AND
COLOR HAT. ATTACH ONE
STRIP OF CONSTRUCTION
PAPER TO EACH END AND
STAPLE. MEASURE CORRECT
SIZE OF CHILD'S HEAD AND
THEN STAPLE STRIP ENDS
TOGETHER. THIS WOULD
BE FUN TO MAKE AFTER
LEARNING THE BASIC
SHAPES OR AFTER PLAYING
THE "SILLY SHAPES" GAME.